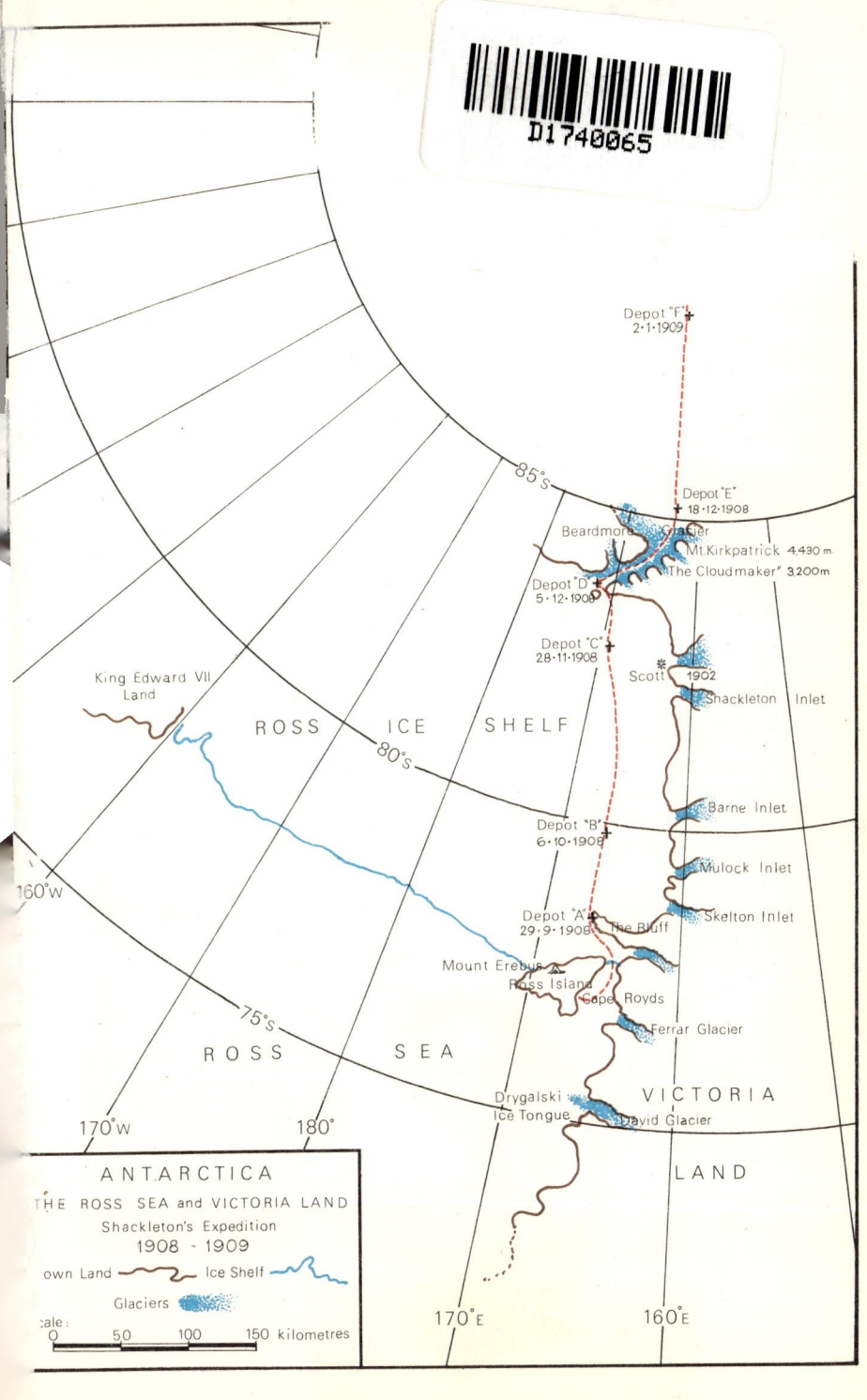

Depot "F"
2·1·1909

Depot "E"
18·12·1908

Beardmore Glacier
Mt.Kirkpatrick 4,430 m
"The Cloudmaker" 3,200m

Depot "D"
5·12·1908

Depot "C"
28·11·1908

Scott 1902

Shackleton Inlet

King Edward VII
Land

ROSS   ICE   SHELF

85°S

80°S

Barne Inlet

Depot "B"
6·10·1908

Mulock Inlet

Skelton Inlet

160°W

Depot "A"
29·9·1908   The Bluff

Mount Erebus
Ross Island

Cape Royds

Ferrar Glacier

75°S

ROSS   SEA

VICTORIA

Drygalski
Ice Tongue   David Glacier

170°W   180°

LAND

170°E   160°E

ANTARCTICA

THE ROSS SEA and VICTORIA LAND

Shackleton's Expedition
1908 - 1909

own Land ⌇⌇⌇   Ice Shelf ⌇⌇⌇

Glaciers

Scale:
0   50   100   150 kilometres

ANTARCTICA
THE HEROIC AGE

Antarctica
The Heroic Age

GEORGE FINKEL

COLLINS Sydney · London

© GEORGE FINKEL 1976

First published 1976 by William Collins Publishers Pty Ltd, Sydney
Type set by Queensland Type Service Pty Ltd, Brisbane
Printed by Dai Nippon Printing Co. (Hong Kong) Ltd

ISBN 0 00 195026 6

Contents

Illustrations

The Background

ONE HUNDRED AND FIFTY years ago men knew less about Antarctica than we know about the far face of the moon.

Until 1774 many armchair geographers believed in a Great Southern Continent, which they thought must exist to balance the landmasses of the Northern Hemisphere. Many old charts show this fancied continent often in great detail. It was shown as being separated from South America by a narrow strait, stretching right across the South Pole, with New Guinea as an outlying cape extending almost to the Equator.

After the voyages of such navigators as Abel Tasman and William Dampier, during the seventeenth century, this huge fancied continent shrank back towards the Antarctic Circle and reality. It was not finally disproved until January 1774 when Captain James Cook had crossed the Antarctic Circle in four widely separated places, being the first navigator to do this. He sailed 480 km beyond the Circle to 70° 48′ S and then was compelled to return by a belt of heavy pack-ice.

I will not say it was impossible anywhere to get further to the South, but attempting it would have been a dangerous and rash enterprise . . . thick fogs, intense cold, and every other thing which can render navigation dangerous, must be encountered . . . if any ports of the land to the South should be open, a ship entering them would run the risk of being fixed [in the ice] there for ever . . .

Cook was certain that land lay to the south, since he reasoned that the enormous icebergs he had sighted must have 'calved' or broken off from glaciers formed ashore. He was quite right about the risks that would be run by ships venturing further to the south. Right into the present century ships have been beset in the pack-ice, some to be held for months, even years, others to be utterly destroyed.

Yet Cook's adverse opinion of Antarctic waters did not prevent other captains from venturing to the south. The reason they went was not exploration, but trade and profit. They were hunting whales – and later seals – for the oil which could be extracted from the thick coating of blubber these animals grow.

There was no mineral oil in use at that time, and the only oils and greases used were either of animal or vegetable origin. Whale oil, as well as being used in lamps for lighting, also had many industrial uses. Whales had been hunted in the Arctic since the days of the Vikings, now the population of Europe was increasing, and the late eighteenth century saw the beginning of the Industrial Revolution; all this added to an increase in the demand for whale oil, and whales were becoming scarce in northern waters. The whaleships were forced to go further and further afield in their search for oil.

Fifty years after James Cook's voyage whaling captains like Balleny, Biscoe and Weddell were sailing 300 km further south than the explorer in their search for whale oil. They gave their names to the new seas they sailed and the islands they found. In 1819–20 three captains, Smith, Bransfield and Palmer, working independently, discovered the South Shetland Islands and two separate stretches of coast; the Palmer and the Trinity Coasts.

There were a number of other discoveries made about this time, but later explorations did not always confirm these. The light can play odd tricks with the eyes in those parts, and as Cook had noted fogs are frequent. Many of the enormous Antarctic icebergs, some have been measured up to 70 km in length, had all the appearance of solid land, especially to seamen who had only seen the much smaller and fantastically pinnacled icebergs of the Arctic.

A little later explorers from Europe and America were sailing Antarctic waters. Unlike Cook, these men had southern bases to support them, for Australia was now settled and ships could winter and refit in Sydney or Hobart. At several points the coast of what we now know to be an Antarctic continent was sighted. In 1840 Sir James Ross discovered the sea and the ice shelf named after him, and called the only active volcano so far discovered in the far south Mount Erebus, after one of his ships. He placed on the charts about 800 km of mountainous coast, which he named Victoria Land, in honour of the young Queen of England.

A Frenchman, Dumont d'Urville, sighted a coast to the east and named it Adélie Land in honour of his wife. An American, Charles Wilkes, discovered another stretch of coast which now bears his name. While a Russian captain, Fabian von Bellingshausen, was the first to sail the dangerous sea named after him.

In the 1840's interest waned in the Antarctic, as explorers turned their attention to the Arctic and the mysterious interior of Africa. Between 1842 and 1892 only one event of interest occurred in these high southern latitudes. In 1873 H.M.S. *Challenger*, a survey ship on a scientific world cruise, became the first ship with steam-power to venture into Antarctic waters across the magic Circle. This was almost exactly one hundred years after James Cook had crossed it for the first time.

Except for *Challenger*'s brief sortie all the exploration in the Antarctic up to that time had been done by sailing ships. By the 1890's steampower was becoming the rule rather than the exception at sea. Steamships had been built since the 1820's, but the early ones had been extravagant of fuel and on long passages relied heavily on sail. By 1890 improvements in steam technology had made the engines both more economical and more reliable, so that steamships – though still helped out in these cases by some sail – could be used to explore the dangerous Antarctic seas.

The poet John Masefield has one of his characters say: 'The man that would go to sea for fun would go to Hell for pastime!'. If this remark has any truth in it, it is true of the approaches to Antarctica. The continent may only be reached through the Roaring Forties and the Furious Fifties, an ocean belt running almost unbroken round the world, where winds of gale force blowing from the west are the rule rather than the exception. Then the explorer's ship must weave its way through a wide belt of pack-ice. In the Ross Sea area the passage through this took an average of eight days, but on one occasion took nearly three weeks. Once in the Ross Sea the expedition had to land its stores, set up a base and the ship leave again within eight weeks, or risk being frozen in for the winter.

On the other side of the continent, in the Weddell Sea, the pack-ice is worse than in the Ross Sea. The explorer who ventured here at the turn of the century was fortunate to sight the coast at all, much less make a landing.

After about 1890 whaleships began to return to the Antarctic. Steam made the ships more manoeuvrable, and the harpoon-gun made the whales easier prey. The whale oil trade had declined since mineral oil came into use in the 1860's, but now new uses were being found, not only for the oil but for the flesh and bones of the whale. Between 1892 and 1895, four Norwegian and one British expedition sailed for Antarctica, seeking whales, but intending to explore as well.

The only respectable length of coastline on the charts, and the most accessible, was that of Victoria Land in the Ross Sea. It had one feature rare in other parts of Antarctica – once a ship was through the belt of floating pack-ice, the Ross Sea was a reasonably calm though chilly lake through the short summer and remarkably free of drifting ice. It was here that the first men landed in Antarctica, at Possession Island off Victoria Land in January 1895. They were from the Norwegian ship *Antarctic*, commanded by Captain Henrik Bull.

This feat proved very little, for no one yet had made a journey into the interior to find out what lay behind the scattered sightings. There could be a continent larger than Australia, which was the most favoured theory among geographers, or it might be an archipelago of large islands bonded into a mass by ice, like nuts in a bar of chocolate.

Of one thing all were certain. Human life in Antarctica could be maintained only with difficulty, and would probably prove to be impossible without supplies of food and fuel from the outside world.

There were scientists who thought that this great natural refrigerator bred the weather for the Southern Hemisphere, and that a study of Antarctic conditions might solve the mystery of the monsoon season. Terrestrial magnetism still held many mysteries, and here was a place where the South Magnetic Pole might be studied on the spot. In the mysterious interior there might be creatures new to science, there might even be a new race of men in some sheltered valley. There might be anything at all.

A Belgian explorer, Captain Adrien de Gerlache, organized the first purely scientific expedition of the Heroic Age in 1897. Some of his ship's company were Norwegian, including a young man named Roald Amundsen. De Gerlache chose to explore the Bellingshausen Sea, but he started late in the season and was frozen into the pack-ice. After drifting for months the crew managed to free the ship and returned to Europe in 1899. They had gained nothing except a lot of experience of ice conditions.

In 1898 Sir George Newnes, a wealthy English publisher, who had taken a great interest in Arctic exploration financed an expedition to Victoria Land which was led by Carstens Borchgrevink, a Norwegian who was working as a surveyor in Queensland. It sailed with a new and daring concept; to find a suitable spot on the coast of Victoria Land where a party could land and build a hut to live in through the winter. To avoid being frozen in the ship would leave and sail north, to spend the southern winter in Australia or New Zealand.

The shore party was landed at Cape Adare and duly wintered, but found it impossible to climb the cliffs that hemmed in their narrow beach, so they could attempt no inland travel. During the winter the biologist to the party, Nicolai Hanson, died of an internal complaint, and became the first person to be buried in Antarctica.

During the next summer the ship, *Southern Cross*, arrived to take the wintering party back to Europe. Though they had made no journeys, the expedition had learned a great deal about the winter climate and conditions. They had proved that men could survive a winter where the sun did not shine for weeks on end, and there the temperature could drop to −60°C.

The Newnes Expedition illustrates the difference reliable steampower had made to Antarctic exploration. Under sail alone no ship could have been sure of battering its way through the pack-ice to pick up a party left ashore the season before, while the dangers of being frozen in had been shown when de Gerlache had been beset in his ship, *Belgica*. Conditions were quite different in the Arctic, where parties had often allowed their ships to be frozen into some sheltered inlet for the winter. But the Arctic is a frozen sea surrounded by continents, while the Antarctic proved to be a glacial continent surrounded by icy seas.

Why the Heroic Age?

The Greeks of the classical world believed that there were beings half-man and half-god, whom they called Heroes. They were endowed with strength and fortitude far beyond that of common man, and could perform mighty feats of endurance beyond human capacity. The men who journeyed to the Antarctic at the beginning of this century seem to me to be true heroes in the latter sense.

This period lasted only from 1901 to 1914, when the outbreak of World War I ended it. During this period all the journeys in the Antarctic were made on foot, some lasting for months and covering distances up to 2560 km. Some were made by men alone, but others were made with the assistance of dogs or ponies. Apart from the steamship which landed them, machinery was never a factor in these journeys. While in the ships the coal fuel used under the boilers was fed in by stokers, using only shovels and muscle power.

None of the ships used exceeded 700 tonnes, about the size of a very small coastal steamer or large ferry today. Some were much smaller, and most were dangerously overloaded when they left the last civilized port. They plunged straight into a voyage across the stormiest ocean in the world, to face a passage through grinding pack-ice at the end of it.

They took no radio, neither in the ships, or the base, nor in the field. Ship-to-ship and ship-to-shore radio was being used during this period, but it was too fragile and cumbersome to be carried in small ships. Towards the end of this period Sir Douglas Mawson succeeded in establishing radio contact between his base in Adélie Land and Pennant Hills near Sydney, Australia, but he often had to use a relay station on Macquarie Island and could never get his signals out in daylight. So communication was neither reliable nor regular.

Radio could have availed them little, in any case. The sailing season to the Ross Sea is short, about ten weeks between the last week in December to the first week in March. This is the period of almost continuous daylight in those latitudes, when radio communication then was rarely possible. Mawson took radio into Antarctica as a scientific experiment, not expecting it to be of any practical use. The four expeditions in this book did not bother with it, knowing it could not help them. Once their ships left the final port of call they were cut off from the rest of the world, and once a sledge party left the base it was entirely on its own.

So these expeditions moved on muscle power: ponymuscle; dog-muscle; and their own muscles. Two expeditions tried motor sledges, without success. Even in temperate countries the internal combustion engine of seventy years ago was far from reliable and not until 1928 was it to become a factor in Antarctic exploration. No one had ever flown an aeroplane at the beginning of this period, and they remained mechanically unreliable at the end.

It is not unreasonable to hail as Heroes in the classical sense men who challenged a frozen world, with a sunless winter lasting for months and no real summer at all. There were many expeditions during this fourteen-year period, and in this book we look at four of them. They have been chosen because in the first, and perhaps the greatest of them, Robert Falcon Scott pioneered a method of Antarctic travel and developed it into a means of making long land journeys. Ernest Henry Shackleton had served under Scott, and later led three expeditions to the south himself, pioneering a practical route to the South Pole and climbing Antarctic mountains for the first time. Roald Amundsen served a long apprenticeship in polar exploration before he went to the Antarctic, discovered a second route to the South Pole and with four companions, Norwegian like himself, reached the Pole in December 1911. At the same time Scott, who had set up a base 650 km distant from the Norwegians', travelled to the Pole by the route Shackleton had found, reaching it a month after Amundsen's party. Scott and his four companions all died on the return journey to their base.

While it is easy to understand why men go to such places as the Antarctic once – the impulse to see what lies over the crest of the next hill is irresistible to many of us – it is not so easy to find the motives why anyone should return to such a barren and inhospitable place. Yet some returned again and again. Frank Wild, who went first as a seaman with Scott, spent eight of the fourteen years covered by this review in South Polar regions.

THE NATIONAL ANTARCTIC EXPEDITION

1901–1904

Robert Falcon Scott

THE SHIP

Discovery

Tonnage	485	Length	52.50 m
Power	325 kW	Draft	5.25 m
Speed	Maximum 8 knots (15.5 km/h)	Beam	10.50 m
	under steam and sail		

THE MEN

Robert Falcon Scott, RN *Leader*
First Lieut. A.B. Armitage*, RNR
F. E. Dailey, RN *Carpenter*
C. A. Ford, RN *Steward*
H. T. Ferrar *Geologist*
Sub-Lieut. G. F. A. Mulock, RNR
Sub-Lieut. E. H. Shackleton, RNR
E. A. Wilson *Surgeon, Geologist*
Lieut. R. W. Skelton, RN *Engineer*
Lieut. M. Barne, RN
L. C. Bernacchi* *Physicist*
J. H. Delbridge, RN *Engineer*

T. H. Feather, RN *Bos'n*
T. V. Hodgson *Biologist*
R. Koettlitz *Botanist*
Lieut. C. W. R. Royds, RN
D. Allen *Petty Officer*
J. Cross *Petty Officer*
E. Evans *Petty Officer*
T. Kennar *Petty Officer*
W. Smythe *Petty Officer*
A. H. Blisset, RM
G. Scott, RM

Seamen

J. Bonner†	G. Croucher	T. Crean
J. Dell	J. Handsley	F. Hare
W. Heald	E. Joyce	A. Pilbeam
W. Vinco†	W. Weller	F. Wild
W. Lashly	F. Plumley	A. Quartley
G. Clarke *Cook*	T. Williamson	T. Whitfield

* Served on earlier Expedition
† Died during Expedition

2

The Young Lieutenant

In 1887 Sir Clements Markham, who was a senior public servant in the India Office, was cruising in the West Indies as the guest of his cousin who was Commodore of the Sail Training Squadron. At that time all young naval officers had to spend some time in sailing ships, and on board H.M.S. *Active* on this cruise was a midshipman, eighteen years of age, whose name was Scott.

Robert Falcon Scott, or Con, as he was known to his family, was duly promoted to Sub-Lieutenant and stationed at Esquimault in Canada. From there he returned to England, intending to specialize in torpedoes. These were new weapons in those days and his intention to specialize in them indicates that Scott was of a scientific turn of mind.

Promoted again, Lieutenant Scott completed his course and went in command of a torpedo boat. His naval career up to then was typical of a young man of a well-to-do family. His father owned an estate and could afford to grant an allowance to Scott and his brother, an Army officer, to supplement their pay.

Suddenly all this was changed. Scott senior went bankrupt and lost all his property, then died three years later. Scott's sisters had to find work, which was not easy seventy-five years ago. His brother left his English regiment and transferred to the West African Frontier Force in Nigeria, where the pay was higher but the service more dangerous. He died of fever only one year later, and Robert Falcon Scott remained, the sole support of his mother and an unmarried sister.

From then on Scott's thoughts were never far from the subject of financial security. Pay was poor in the junior ranks of the Navy and peacetime promotion was slow. While his family had been well-to-do these things had not mattered. Now they did, and to Scott an early promotion and the consequent increase in pay seemed vital.

In the spring of 1899 Scott was a lieutenant, thirty years of age, with a hope of being promoted to Commander in a few years time. While on leave in London he met Sir Clements Markham, who was now President of the Royal Geographical Society, who recognized Scott as the midshipman he had known years before.

They happened to be walking in the same direction, and Scott learned for the first time that the Society was planning to send an expedition into the Antarctic. He had never thought of becoming an explorer, but now he saw a chance of making a name for himself. Sir Clements has told us that even as a midshipman Scott had shown exceptional powers of leadership, and that twelve years before he had marked Scott as a possible commander of a polar expedition. Scott applied to command the National Antarctic Expedition, and was so appointed.

Knowing the circumstances it was not difficult to see why he did this. The most important promotion in a naval officer's career is to commander's rank. Normally this occurs between the ages of thirty-one and thirty-five, a period known as the *promotion zone*. Any officer passing through this zone without being promoted has very little chance of being advanced afterwards.

Scott was promoted to commander on being appointed to lead the expedition, taking up his new duty in February 1900. He could expect to be absent in the south for two or three years, and the results of the expedition were almost entirely up to him. If it were a success he could expect a decoration, possibly even a knighthood, on his return. His promotion to captain was almost a certainty in that case, as the navy was beginning its greatest peacetime expansion in history. For Robert Falcon Scott the future seemed bright indeed.

Today an expedition such as Scott was to lead would be paid for entirely by the Government, but the National Antarctic Expedition was a private venture launched by the Royal Geographical Society. It was Sir Clements Markham, himself an explorer in his earlier years, who set about raising the money and equipment needed. Business firms or scientific societies might contribute by donating supplies or the loan of equipment, but the money had to be literally begged for. As it has today for charities like the Freedom from Hunger campaign, or UNICEF.

£90,000 was needed. Sir Clements was promised half of this by the Government if the Society could raise the other half. They did rather better than this, raising £47,000 about the time that Scott took up his duties. The Government doubled this, so on this expedition Scott had no financial worries.

A wooden ship was being built, fitted with steam-engines but also rigged for sail. This steam-and-sail combination strikes us as odd today, but the men who were to sail in *Discovery*, as she was named, would not think so. Steam-and-sail gunboats were in use in the Persian Gulf and along the East African coast for some years after this.

Discovery was built of wood for two reasons. It was intended to carry out a programme of magnetic research, and the instruments would be less affected by a wooden hull. Also it was felt that a wooden ship would stand the pressure better than one of steel should she be frozen into the ice. Apart from four scientists all but two of the expedition members were from the Royal Navy. Scott preferred it this way because, as he tells us, he had no experience of dealing with civilians.

The expedition was to seek a base in the Ross Sea, while a German expedition led by Professor von Drygalski was to explore a reported coast some hundreds of kilometres to the northwest. The South Magnetic Pole, it was hoped, would lie between their bases and both agreed to share the results of their researches. It was important that they begin their experiments on the same day, and Scott visited the German leader to arrange a programme. He found their preparations for departure much in advance of his own.

A secretary was engaged and an office rented in London, and Scott set to work. He had just over a year to get ready if he was to keep faith with his German colleague. Gradually he was joined by his officers, and they had to think of everything they would need for a three-year absence, with the possible exception of seal or penguin meat. Today if an expedition sails and something has been overlooked a message may be radioed to base and the missing items brought on by aircraft. In 1900 ship-to-shore radio was still in the experimental stage and nothing but primitive balloons had ever left the ground. If anything was forgotten, the expedition would have to manage without it.

There was little to guide Scott in his planning, although there had been many expeditions to the Arctic during the past century. But Arctic experience was no great help, due to the difference in conditions. The Arctic is an open sea surrounded by continents and islands, but there were good reasons for knowing that the Antarctic was a frozen continent with high mountains surrounded by ice. Wherever he goes in the Arctic the explorer finds seals or bears, and he may use the flesh for food and the fat or blubber for fuel. The Esquimau of the north has built a whole culture round the products of these two beasts, for they are all he has.

Away from the coast in Antarctica the explorer must take with him every thing he needs. The land is lifeless as the moon and not much warmer. He cannot even drink unless he first melts the ice, for it is much too cold to suck. A stove and fuel are essential to the traveller if he is not to die of thirst.

The results of the Newnes Expedition three years earlier had few lessons for Scott, since the wintering party had been unable to travel from their hut. Scott and his staff had to work almost everything out from first principles.

The work these young men did in one year was prodigious. The ship was launched and fitted out, stores were bought, catalogued and packed, and tons of instruments and equipment brought together. They sailed in August 1901 and nothing important was forgotten.

In order to keep faith with the Germans, *Discovery* sailed before she was really ready. There had been no time for the usual shakedown cruise with the new ship, followed by a period in the dockyard to make good any defects. In fact, the shakedown cruise was a very long one – a passage to New Zealand by way of the Cape of Good Hope.

Scott was very disappointed with his ship; she was slow

under both sail and steam and used a great deal of fuel. Because of the slowness a deep sea trawling and sounding programme had to be abandoned.

She also had a bad leak. Much time at sea was spent shifting stores in the crowded holds trying to find the leak from the inside. But *Discovery* had been built with three layers of planking, so the place where the hull leaked on the inside might be a long way from where the water got in on the outside. At Simonstown Dockyard in South Africa *Discovery* was unloaded and drydocked. This did something, but the leak was still bad.

No captain could be easy in his mind when about to leave for the stormiest seas in the world with a leaking ship. Scott made the best of a bad job, and left for the southward to begin the magnetic observations to keep faith with Professor von Drygalski. These began while the ship was on passage between the Cape and Port Lyttelton in New Zealand.

Here the ship was unloaded and drydocked twice, still without tracing the leak. *Discovery* sailed from Port Lyttelton on Christmas Eve, with the ship's company increased by forty-five sheep and twenty-three dogs. The sailing had been delayed a day by the tragic death of a young seaman named Bonner, who climbed to the main-truck and tried to balance himself on the very tip of the masthead. He lost his footing and was killed when he fell to the deck.

The sheep were to be slaughtered as soon as the ship reached the pack-ice, when the meat would be preserved by the cold. The dogs were either survivors or descendants of the Newnes Expedition, and were to be used for transport.

It is strange that Scott had not thought of using dogs

before this. He had been in Canada, where dog sleds are still used as winter transport. Right through his career as an explorer Scott seems to have disliked the idea of using dogs for haulage. Perhaps he was influenced by accounts of man-hauled sledge journeys in the Arctic during the mid-nineteenth century, for in his *Journal* he several times comments on the nobility of such journeys unassisted by animals.

Scott was a most humane man, and long journeys by dog sled can call for a certain amount of ruthlessness. Weaker dogs may have to be sacrificed to provide food for stronger ones, or even for their human drivers.

The Expedition had an easy passage to the Ross Sea. The first icebergs were sighted on 2 January 1902, and as earlier voyagers had noted they were huge compared to the icebergs in the Arctic. The next day they crossed the Antarctic Circle (66°30' S.) and entered the pack-ice.

This is a belt of floating ice varying in width and extending right round Antarctica. It is formed of the ice that freezes over the sea in winter becoming broken up in spring and floating off to the north. Sometimes one or more layers are driven over one another by the wind, then they freeze together and are said to have rafted. Small bergs become frozen into it also, and it is a great danger to ships in the autumn, when many have been 'beset', or frozen in to form part of the pack itself. It was now the Antarctic midsummer and the pack-ice was at its loosest and most broken. Under steam the ship could force her way through, though only very slowly.

It was daylight through the twenty-four hours. Now the sheep were slaughtered and the carcasses hung in the rigging to freeze. Seals and penguins were sunning themselves on the icefloes, and some of these were shot as food for the dogs. Seal meat was tried by the human explorers, and at first it was not liked. Later it was eaten with pleasure and seal liver became a looked-for delicacy, as did penguin breast. Once the base was established the dogs were given nothing but seal meat and they thrived on it.

James Cook had feared that his ships might become beset in the ice, and the thought must have been in the front of Commander Scott's mind too. But this did not happen, their progress southwards was slow but sure. It was found that the upper part of the small bergs trapped in the pack melted down into pure water, quite free of salt, so the water tanks were filled from this source. They had brought Norwegian skis with them, and made the first experiments with these on the smoother floes. To all except Scott and the ship's officers the passage through the pack-ice was a holiday.

In four days they were through the pack-ice and had entered into the open waters of the Ross Sea. Commander Scott set a course for Cape Adare, where the Newnes Expedition had wintered four years earlier. He was interested in finding out if the hut they had built was still in existence.

3

Hut Point

DISCOVERY arrived off Cape Adare on 9 January 1902, sixteen days out from Port Lyttelton. Though it was midsummer, Commander Scott knew that he had only eight or ten weeks to find a base before the sea froze over again.

Bernacchi, the physicist, had been one of the men who had wintered at Cape Adare, and found his old home still in good condition. Scott soon decided that it was useless for his expedition, for the frozen cliffs surrounding it prevented any travel towards the hinterland.

So they stayed there only one day, but before leaving Scott had a message nailed in a sealed container to the door of the hut. In the days before radio this was the only way an explorer could communicate with a possible search party, by leaving a message at a known point.

He went on, coasting along Victoria Land's mountainous shores without finding a spot for a base. On 21 January he entered McMurdo Strait, between Victoria Land and Ross Island. At that time it was thought to be a sound, and Ross Island was believed to be a peninsula.

Ross Island is a splendid landmark and had been discovered by Sir James Clark Ross over sixty years before. On it are two volcanoes, one of which is still active. They were named after the ships of the Ross Expedition, Erebus and Terror. Mount Erebus the active one, is 4270 m high, while Mount Terror is only slightly lower.

The Sound was choked with ice but this was breaking up fast and streaming northward under the summer sun. The Sound seemed a good place to set up a base as soon as it was free from ice, so while he waited for this, Scott took the ship round to Cape Crozier on the other side of the island. Here he had arranged to leave a second message.

Since leaving New Zealand the magnetic experiments had been going on and while the ship was off Cape Crozier Scott, with Wilson and Royds, made his first excursion on shore. They walked a few kilometres inland and climbed 425 m up the slopes of Mount Terror. There was little to see, only the featureless expanse of the Ross Ice Shelf.

This is the largest floating Ice Shelf in the world. It is attached to land on three sides and stretches 730 km along its northern edge. Many of the huge Antarctic icebergs are born here as pieces of the floating edge breaking off under their own weight. Sir James Ross had sailed 640 km along it to the east without finding where it ended.

This discovery was left for Scott. With his engines he was able to press farther east than Ross, and eighty kilometres beyond the earlier explorers' limit he found the first new land discovered in the twentieth century. It was an icebound coast backed by a low range of mountains, but he was unable to land. Scott named it King Edward VII Land and the Queen Alexandra Mountains in honour of the newly crowned rulers of Britain.

Scott would have liked to base the expedition here, but streams of heavy pack-ice prevented a landing. So he turned back towards McMurdo Strait, finding on the way a curious bay in the Ice Shelf, where he stayed three days.

The height of this Shelf ranged between thirty and seventy-five metres, but in this bay the ice dropped almost to sea-level and the ship was able to moor alongside as if at a quay in a civilized port. While Armitage and Bernacchi took a sledge and a party of seamen towards the south, Scott prepared to make a balloon ascent to look for signs of land.

Hydrogen gas in cylinders had been brought to inflate the balloon, which rose to a height of 244 m on the end of a cable. Scott and Shackleton (the expedition photographer) made two ascents, seeing nothing but their shipmates steadily trekking south. Then the wind rose and the balloon had to be hauled down, not to be used again because of the lack of hydrogen.

The landing party travelled eleven kilometres then camped for the night. Armitage and a seaman went south next day while Bernacchi did some magnetic experiments. This journey of sixteen kilometres over the Ice Shelf does not sound very much but it was important. It had proved that men could travel over the ice and survive a night with only a tent and sleeping bags for shelter.

They had found sledging to be slower, than they had thought, and sledge-hauling to be hard work. At very low temperatures ice becomes gritty and hauling a sledge over it is like hauling it over gravel.

On 8 February they were again in McMurdo Strait, with only about five weeks before the freeze up to find a base. A place was found on the west side of Ross Island and Scott was faced with a big decision. Should he set up the huts he had brought and land a small party, sending the rest back with the ship to winter in New Zealand? Or should he allow the ship to be frozen in and keep the expedition together?

He decided on the latter, as many explorers in the Arctic had done in the past. Topmasts and yards were struck down, and a canvas awning extended from bow to stern over the upper deck. The boilers were emptied and the engines greased. The ship had been built so that rudder and propeller could be disconnected and drawn up into the hull, to prevent them from being crushed by ice, and this was done.

In five weeks the ship was frozen in. During this time the huts were unloaded and set up on shore. There were three of these, the largest intended as living quarters for a shore party, but it was used as a storeroom and recreational space. Two smaller huts, with no iron in their construction, were used for magnetic research. The site was named Hut Point, and still appears on today's maps under this name.

Now the first experiments were made with dog-driving, an art difficult to acquire since none of the men had ever driven a dog-team and none of the dogs had ever been driven. But in a week or two dogs were hauling supplies up the beach alongside their human shipmates, and Scott was planning a journey overland to Cape Crozier, to bring the message left there up to date.

This was 145 km across the ice and Scott hoped to learn a great deal from this journey. He had intended to lead the party, but while practising on skis he had torn a tendon and could scarcely walk. So Royds was put in charge and set off on 4 March with twelve men and eight dogs.

After four days of floundering through soft snow Royds had to revise this plan. The surface was suitable for skis but they had only three pairs of them. Royds decided to press on for Cape Crozier with the two best skiers and one sledge, and send the others back to the ship in charge of Barne.

On 9 March Royds went on with Dr Koettlitz and Lieut. Skelton, while the others turned back. Two days later Barne's party reached a square-topped hill named Castle Rock, which was only five kilometres from the ship. Here they had to leave the smooth ice and clamber over rocky slopes, and Barne ordered the men to change their finneskoe for the nailed ski boots they carried with them. Finneskoe are Norwegian reindeer fur snow boots, the soles being made of skin from the head or foreleg of the animal, the short stiff hair providing a good grip on the ice.

All the men did this except Vince and Hare, who had packed their ski boots carelessly and these were now crushed flat and frozen stiff. Suddenly a blizzard came up and they lost sight of the ship. Almost blinded by driving snow they pitched the tents and made camp.

They had two stoves but both had broken down, so they could neither prepare a meal nor melt snow for a drink. Later on Barne would have known that the best thing to do would be to stay where he was until the weather cleared, for men have been lost within a few paces of their hut in an Antarctic blizzard. But they were all still learning, and Barne decided to make for the ship in case they became too weak to travel.

They set out, leaving the tent and sledges to be collected later. After some time they found that Hare, one of the two still wearing finneskoe, was missing, and while searching for him Barne and two seamen fell down an icefall. They were unhurt but could not climb back to rejoin the others. They sheltered in a rock cranny to wait for the blizzard to blow itself out.

The five men still at the top of the icefall included a young seaman called Frank Wild. Wild was to spend most of the next twenty years in the Antarctic, and to make a great name for himself. He took charge of the party, but Vince, the other man wearing finneskoe, lost his footing and he too went over a cliff. Wild led the others safely back to the ship and made his report.

Scott, still unable to walk, organized search-parties at once. Delbridge, the engineer, raised steam and the melancholy sound of the ship's siren echoed over the icy scene. Three hours later Armitage found Barne and two seamen, and guided them back to the ship. All three were hungry and frostbitten.

That left Vince and Hare still missing, and both were given up for lost. Then, next day, Hare arrived on board. He had not eaten for forty hours nor had a drink for sixty hours, yet he soon recovered. Hare had found it impossible to stand in finneskoe, he had called out his intention to return to the tent and have another go at putting on his boots but no one had heard him, and Barne thought he had gone over the cliff.

Finding he could not reach the tent, Hare had crept into a small cave and was drifted over with snow and fell asleep. When he awoke the weather was clear and he managed to reach the ship. Vince's body was never found.

Royds returned to base on 19 March, having failed to reach Cape Crozier because of weather. Wisely Scott made no further attempts to bring the message at Cape Crozier up to date until the next spring because he knew no ship could reach it until January 1903 at the earliest. But he made one more short journey before suspending all travel until the next season.

This was a four-day journey which he led himself. With three companions he travelled through a passage called The Gap on to the surface of the Ice Shelf. There were no mistakes this time – Scott was learning how to travel in Antarctica. In this first expedition he never made the same mistake twice.

4

The First Winter

In April 1902 Hut Point was a busy place. The ship was almost entirely frozen in, stores were stacked above high water mark, and three huts stood on the shore. The harsh outlines of man-made things were being softened by drifting snow. There were shouts and yelping dogs, bloodstains from slaughtered seals, drifting smoke and the smell of cooking. The Antarctic was to see many such scenes over the next twelve years.

Commander Scott had a great deal to think about; although the passage down had been successful and he had secured a firm base from which to strike inland, two men had died. Bonner's death was something that might happen to any foolhardy seaman showing off, but he could not help blaming himself for the death of Vince. Such a thing must not happen again.

Scott was a naval officer, responsible for the men under him, although in some cases they might be older than himself. He knew that sailors tend to be careless of clothing issued to them and Vince's carelessness in packing his boots had indirectly caused his death.

Another factor was the failure of the stoves. These were primus stoves, which had been invented in the 1880's and are still in use. Without such stoves exploration in Antarctica would be impossible, for food is frozen hard as rock and to suck supercooled snow to obtain a drink would be to invite death from a frostbitten throat.

Primus stoves burn vaporized kerosene forced under air pressure through a fine jet, and this jet needs to be cleaned frequently with a fine wire 'pricker' if the stove is to work. Barne had forgotten to bring any of these cleaners with him, so Vince lost his life for want of a pricker worth half a cent.

The lesson was not wasted on Scott. As soon as he returned from his excursion through The Gap he set up a programme to train his men in methods of polar travel. He organized exercises in ski running, sledge packing, man-hauling, dog-driving and camping. Also instructions on the care of sledges, tents, equipment and clothing. There were dog-team races, and competitions in tent pitching and sledge hauling. Not many mistakes were made in the following sledging seasons.

The old Arctic explorers had dreaded the sunless winters, and Scott had not looked forward with any pleasure to that winter of 1902. To his relief it passed busily and happily. Once the huts and stores were landed there was plenty of room on board, with the hut on shore as additional working space. There were few written orders and those mostly devoted to prevent fire breaking out in the wooden ship. Scott ran this expedition by example and found he had little need to give direct orders.

There was no pretence of equality between officers and lower deck, which some have seen as a fault. The two marines acted as officers' servants, but this paid a dividend in that the specialists were able to get on with their work without being distracted by domestic chores. As a result the scientific findings of this expedition were very valuable.

Officers and the lower deck ate in their separate messes, but all ate the same food. Scott has been criticized for maintaining these social differences, but in fact he had no choice because there was nowhere in the ship where all could sit down together, and everyone was probably happier living with his own kind.

The living spaces were heated by anthracite, a variety of hard coal, stoves but the temperatures were never very high. At head level it varied between 4.5° and 10° C, but on deck it rarely rose above freezing point. This was because the decks were not insulated and the cold struck up through them from the unheated and empty spaces below. To keep their feet warm on board everyone wore Russian boots made of thick felt.

The two coldest places in the ship were the galley, which soon iced up from the steam of the cooking, and Scott's cabin and office which backed onto the engine room; this was freezing cold with the engines shut down and no fires in the boilers. Ice formed early on the bulkhead, where it remained until the summer thaw, and Scott worked at his desk with his feet in a box of hay to try and keep them warm.

During the first winter they used kerosene lamps. Attempts were made to use a wind-driven generator to provide lighting current, but this was wrecked in an autumn blizzard. During the second winter acetylene gas was used for lighting. A generator to produce this had been taken to light the hut if it were used to house a wintering party. It gave a very soft clear light and most expeditions during the Heroic Age made use of it.

On board officers and men wore long woollen underwear and blue trousers tucked into felt boots, lambswool vests and flannel shirts. Over this the officers wore cardigans and the lower deck, jerseys. Scott did not use fur clothing, except for the hands and feet, and the trail dress consisted of trousers and blouse of windproof gaberdine with balaclava helmets and windproof hoods. Trail footwear consisted of a few pair of lambswool socks, with finneskoe stuffed with saengrass for travel over ice or ski boots for travel over rock. Saengrass is a dried Arctic plant with a great capacity for absorbing moisture, and was used here to absorb perspiration from the feet.

Hands were protected by a pair of silk gloves, then woollen mittens, with dogskin gauntlets over all. These last had no divisions between the fingers, only the thumb being separate. To lose a gauntlet was to risk losing a finger by frostbite, so they were slung round the neck on a harness made from cotton lampwick.

Frostbite in Antarctica is much commoner than sunstroke in the tropics. At first it is painless, no more than a gradual loss of sensation. The flesh goes white and hard, and on the trail men regularly examine each other's faces for signs of it. The pain comes as it thaws, leaving a blister like a severe burn. More than one traveller in the Heroic Age lost toes by frostbite.

The trail tents were very light, made of grenfell cloth like the windproof clothing, and were gradually modified until they became a strong and reliable shelter. Sleeping bags were of reindeer fur and at first Scott used bags to sleep three men, but in the second year he changed over to separate one-man bags.

Most sailors in those days were handy with their needles, and alterations to the dress and tents and the manufacture of sleeping bags kept many of them busy. As well as these tasks there were ration packs to be made up and dogs to exercise and train. No one had time to become bored.

The scientific staff had their researches to keep them busy, while the officers looked after the smooth running of the ship and ran the various departments. Weather readings were taken every two hours during the entire period the ship was at Hut Point, the officers, including Scott, taking it in turns to act as night watchman and note the night readings. One of the privileges of this task was that the watchman could heat two pails of water on the galley stove and take a bath between two sets of readings.

Monday to Friday were working days, Saturday forenoon was clean-ship day and the afternoon was a make-and-mend, the naval term for a half-holiday. On Sunday forenoons Scott inspected the whole ship and held a short service afterwards. New Zealand mutton was served for Sunday dinner, while it lasted, with another make-and-mend in the afternoon

Shackleton had already published one book and now started a monthly magazine, the *South Polar Times*. This began a tradition which lasted throughout the period of British expeditions. All contributions were anonymous and there was a great deal of speculation about the authorship of some of the more scandalous articles!

Bernacchi and Armitage were the only members of the expedition with previous cold climate experience. Bernacchi had wintered at Cape Adare, and Lieut. Armitage had been to Spitzbergen. Armitage was the only one with experience of sledge travel, having crossed Spitzbergen eight years before.

Scott's stoves, cookers and sledges varied little from those in use today, and had all been developed by the Norwegian Arctic explorer, Fridtjof Nansen. The sledges were about three and a half metres long by half a metre wide. The runners were split not sawn, from English ash, turned up at each end like skis. No nails or screws were used, the joints being mortised and tenoned and bound with copper wire. The result was a sledge weighing only twenty kilos, strong and flexible enough to carry a 500 kg load over a rough icy surface for hundreds of miles.

Scott's travel plans were based on three-man trail units. This meant that he had certain fixed weights to carry on the sledge: the tent and floorcloth, the sleeping bag, the stove and cooker. With tools and instruments this came to about 135 kg, including the sledge itself, which could increase by 20 per cent as the tent and sleeping bag iced up.

Trail rations were one kilo of concentrated food per man per day, in containers holding three-man rations for a week. With supplies for a six-week journey a sledge weighed about 375 kg on setting out, about the limit a three-man team could pull.

Thus, the length of a journey was limited by the amount the sledge team could pull, as the range of a steamship was limited by the amount of coal in her bunkers. This latter case was a familiar one to Scott and his officers, but he could not solve his sledging problem as he solved the coal problem with a ship which called at fuelling stations scattered about the sealanes of the world. The only means to extend an Antarctic journey was either lay depots along the route in advance, or to use supporting parties to assist in advancing the main effort.

There are several ways of doing this. A party may leave the base with supplies for a six-week journey, travel for ten days in the intended direction, then depot four weeks' supplies. They then have four days' food with which to reach the base, making a gamble that the return trip with a lightened sledge will take them only half the time. After a short rest and reprovisioning at the base they can then set out again with a full load, provisioned for a ten-week journey.

This can be further extended by using supporting parties. Twelve men (four parties) set out from base, picking up full loads from a depot laid earlier two weeks' journey out. At regular intervals a supporting party returns, taking with it only sufficient food to reach the base and leaving a depot for the other three parties to do likewise. When the main party reached its turning point there would be a string of depots between it and the base, each containing sufficient food to last them to the next depot. Journeys of up to five months away from base have been made by using these methods.

A disadvantage of the depot and supporting party system is that the main party must follow the same route out and home, which need not be so in these days of trail radios and airdropped supplies. But however it is done Antarctic travel is no occupation for weaklings, and is still as hazardous as any space flight.

5

Scott's Farthest South

SCOTT, with Barne and Shackleton, left on a depot laying journey on 17 September 1902. It was too early for travel, but this was something Scott had to find out. Their tent was wrecked by a blizzard two days later, so they dumped their stores and returned to Hut Point.

Scott set out again a week later at the head of four three-man teams assisted by dogs, to find that mixed man and dog teams did not work. The dogs set a quicker pace than the men, they got in each other's way, and both grew tired more quickly than if the teams were not mixed.

Reaching the Ice Shelf through The Gap, they picked up the loads dumped the week before and steered for a rocky headland known as The Bluff. When they reached this on 1 October six weeks' supplies were left there in a depot marked by a tall stack of ice blocks crowned with a flag. Then the party returned to Hut Point.

It was 136 km from The Bluff to Hut Point and they covered this distance in three days. Scott was jubilant, for such a speed made him hopeful for the Southern Journey towards the Pole. Then Armitage, who had been out with another depot laying party to the west, returned with several men sick with scurvy.

The object of Armitage's journey was to find a pass through the coastal mountains of Victoria Land in an attempt to reach the South Magnetic Pole. The going was very rough and there were many falls among the icy rocks. It was noted that some men bruised more easily than others, and easy bruising is a symptom of scurvy.

The symptoms were confirmed as scurvy by the doctors at Hut Point. Although means of preventing and curing scurvy had been known since the days of James Cook, no one as yet knew the cause. Fresh fruit and vegetables made miraculous recoveries possible and so to a lesser degree did fresh meat and fish. We now know scurvy to be caused by an absence of certain vitamins in the diet, but vitamins had not been discovered in 1902.

Scott's doctors did the correct things to cure the outbreak, but for the wrong reasons. Suspecting that the outbreak was caused by eating preserved meat that had become tainted, Scott had this all destroyed and replaced it with fresh seal meat.

Thinking that crowded living conditions might have some part to play, the ship's interior was thoroughly scrubbed and whitewashed, and one-third of the men took up their quarters in the hut ashore, changing over each week. Dr Koettlitz grew a crop of fresh mustard and cress on damp flannel stretched over frames below the wardskylight, producing enough to provide a good salad for all hands. The sickness disappeared within a fortnight, but from then on the fear of scurvy was always in Scott's mind.

Meanwhile a party of fit men led by Royds had reached Cape Crozier and brought the message there up to date. They came back with a remarkable story. Cape Crozier was a nesting ground for the largest of the penguins, the Emperor, and there was evidence that these birds hatched their eggs in midwinter in the open air without a nest. This was specially interesting to Dr Wilson, who as well as being a medical man was a keen ornithologist.

Most expeditions during the Heroic Age included a few scientists, but the great driving force of the day was geographic discovery. Much of the money they needed was raised by public subscription and the ordinary man was not stirred by the importance of magnetic research or the nesting habits of penguins. What he wanted for his money was the filling in of blank spaces on the map, with tales of fortitude and endurance and the eventual discovery of the South Pole.

Scott knew he had little chance of reaching the Pole on this expedition, but he hoped to get a long way towards it. For all he knew it might be humanly impossible to reach the Pole at all, for men had been trying to reach the North Pole for centuries without success. But he had to try to reach the South Pole, for while he had no orders to do so there was an understanding between himself and the Expedition Committee in England that he would try.

The main Southern Journey began on 30 October, when Barne led four three-man teams towards The Bluff. Three days later Scott, Wilson and Shackleton left Hut Point driving a dog-team, expecting to find Barne's party at The Bluff when they arrived. Instead they caught up with him next day when the party was held up by blizzards and gales. It took them ten days to reach The Bluff.

Reloading the sledges from the depot they set off into the unknown. Scott intended to lay two more depots, then push on with a single team and go as far as he could. They reached 79° south on 13 November, a new 'Farthest South' record, and the first to be set by land travel. Here Scott established Depot A and two of the supporting parties turned back.

The supercooled snow was gritty under the sledge-runners and travel was difficult. The sun was veiled with haze and they seemed to travel in a bowl of white glare, featureless and depressing. One after the other the explorers became snowblind for a few days, with their eyes watering continually and feeling as if they were filled with hot sand. They improvised goggles of wood or leather with a slit cut in them for vision in their attempt to shield themselves from the brilliant glare.

When the sun was invisible they had no guide to direction. The compass was no use at all, for the South Magnetic Pole was now to the northeast of them and the needle tended to point down into the ground. This was because the Geographic and the Magnetic Poles, north and south, are about 1600 km apart, and the magnetic poles move through a regular figure-of-eight pattern. This does not matter much in the tropical and temperate zones, since the rate of movement is known and can be allowed for. But it matters a great deal to the traveller within the Antarctic Circle.

Yet accurate navigation was essential if they were to complete their journey, since to survive they had to be able to find the depots. On rare clear days they could see mountains on the coast of Victoria Land, but they could not rely on having many clear days.

So they learned to steer by the sastrugi, waves in the snow cut by the prevailing winds and frozen hard as concrete. Sastrugi here ran roughly east and west, so they only had to cross them at a certain angle to know they were on the right course.

For reckoning distance they had the sledgemeter. Skelton had invented and built several of these in the ship's machine-shop during the winter. A sledgemeter was a wheel and attached to this was an automatic engine revolution counter from the engine room. Each revolution of the wheel was recorded on the counter, and when the instrument was fixed to the rear of a sledge and set to zero each morning, the day's run could be calculated with accuracy every evening.

So while Scott could not calculate his position by either sun or stars, he had worked out a way of doing so by what sailors call dead reckoning, and which used to be known as navigating 'by guess and by God'!

On 15 November Scott pressed onwards with Shackleton and Wilson, five sledges and the dogs. Five sledges were too many for three men to haul at one time, and they had to use the method which became known as relaying.

Setting off in the morning three sledges were hauled southwards for four kilometres, where one man was left to erect the tent and prepare lunch while the others walked back with the dogs to bring up the remaining two sledges. The process was repeated in the afternoon, so that each day they advanced eight kilometres to the south, but walked twenty-four kilometres to do so. This went on for more than a month.

On 25 November they crossed 80° south and were now literally 'off the map', for the meridional lines on the chart stopped at 80° to leave a blank circle of white paper round the Pole. In clear weather they could still see mountains to the west, but nothing to the south. This made dog-driving difficult, for dogs like something to march towards, and now they had to be forced every step of the way.

On 3 December there was a clear spell and Scott took the bearings of a high mountain he named Mount Longstaff, in honour of one of the supporters of the expedition. The white circle on the chart was blank no longer.

Before this Scott had noted that the dogs were weakening and put this fact down to the food they were eating – dried stockfish, as advised by Nansen. It might also have been due to overwork, for they were still relaying with the dogs doing much of the hauling. On 10 December the first dog died, to be cut up and fed to the others.

Scott then decided he would use the weaker dogs to feed the stronger and made a depot of most of the dog food. For the first time for more than a month they were able to advance without relaying.

Now men as well as dogs were becoming weaker and Dr Wilson thought he detected signs of scurvy in Shackleton. They were not serious and it was some weeks before Shackleton knew he was ill. Again, it was probably the food to blame, but here there was no fresh seal meat or mustard and cress to give relief.

The food was good enough of its kind, but it was all either dried or preserved. The staples were biscuits and pemmican, helped out with peaflour, oatmeal, and a little butter and cheese. Pemmican was made from lean beef, dried and powdered and made into a cake by the addition of fat. It was eaten after being cooked into a thick soup with peaflour and condiments, when it was known as 'hoosh'. Such a diet was high in protein and fats, but almost free of vitamins. As already mentioned, no one knew anything about vitamins at that time.

Lime juice, we know now, as well as cod-liver oil, are both rich in the vitamins which will prevent and cure scurvy, and both had been used for many years, so it seems strange that Scott did not take and use one or the other, especially as the records of the Arctic expeditions frequently mention cases of scurvy.

Because they were eating the wrong food it did not satisfy them and they were hungry all the time. They were also running short of their kerosene fuel, having been too generous in its use at the start. They began eating a cold lunch, lumps of pemmican carried next to their bodies on the march and nibbled as soon as the surface softened a little. Even Christmas Day, with double whacks of everything and a Christmas pudding carried in a spare sock and contributed by Shackleton, failed to satisfy them.

On the last day of 1902 they reached 82°11' south, the limit of their journey and 350 km nearer the Pole than ever man had been before. For a miracle the weather was clear and a mountain far to the south was named Mount Markham in honour of the founder of the expedition. The nearest point of land was named for Wilson and a glacier inlet for Shackleton.

Though he had hoped to go further, Scott had made a magnificent journey. He had pioneered Antarctic land travel and found a practical route towards the south. He had put features onto a blank chart, and traced the coast of Victoria Land 400 km further south. Now he had to get back to tell the world what he had found.

He was beginning to think it would be touch and go if he did this. Twelve dogs had died and the sensible thing to do would have been to shoot the remainder. They had become slow on their feet and were now being helped along by the men. Travel would have speeded up without the dogs, and a few meals of fresh meat would have helped alleviate the scurvy.

By now Shackleton was badly affected and the others were showing the symptoms: loose teeth, bleeding gums and easily bruised flesh. The sledgemeter broke and the metal sheathing of the sledge-runners began to tear away. But they found enough of their outward tracks to guide them to a depot where they had left a spare sledge.

With this as a reserve Scott experimented with the metal-clad sledge-runners. He stripped all the broken metal from one set of runners, and found that bare wood gave a better gliding surface than the metal-clad runners. It was just as well this was so and that the wear on the runners was light, for Shackleton was now so weak he had to be carried on the sledge.

They were nineteen days in this state, two sick men dragging a third on the sledge. In any civilized state all three would have been in hospital.

They reached Hut Point on 3 February 1903. Wilson, the least affected of the three, took a month to recover.

6

The Second Season

DURING SCOTT'S ABSENCE in the south Armitage had taken a party westward, discovered a pass through the coastal mountains towards the plateau of Victoria Land and pressed on towards the region of the South Magnetic Pole. The journey had been quite as difficult as Scott's southern one, although the distance travelled had been much less. Part of the difficulty was that much of the trip lay in a glacier pass and on a plateau 2450 m above sea level, so that Armitage had to combat the effects of altitude as well as those of extreme cold. He travelled a distance of 150 km from Hut Point.

The pass to the plateau was so steep that in some places the men drove crowbars into the ice, lashed pulleys to these and hauled the sledges up on ropes a few metres at a time. On the outward journey they faced continual strong westerly winds, which blistered their faces with a frostbite.

Armitage could have gone further, but he was under orders to have the ship ready for sea by the end of January. He knew he could not reach the South Magnetic Pole with the time he had, so he turned gratefully back to the base on 5 January 1903, his last camp being at a height of 2900 metres. Travelling much faster downhill with the wind behind him, he reached Hut Point on 19 January and when Scott arrived there a fortnight later the ship was almost ready for sea.

Travelling by dog team (Scott 1910–1913) *Popperphoto*

SLEDGING

Hauling by man-power (Scott 1910–1913) *Popperphoto*

'His Master's Voice' (Scott 1910–1913)
Popperphoto

WILD LIFE

Adelie penguin *Popperphoto*

Rookery of Adelie penguins *Popperphoto*

Scott had not intended to spend more than one season in Antarctica, though he knew he might be forced to do so, which was why *Discovery* was provisioned for three years. The Expedition Committee in London were fully aware of the risks he might run, and when *Discovery* did not winter in New Zealand a Relief Expedition was formed to follow his track and assist him as necessary.

Morning, a steam whaler, was chartered and placed under the command of Lieut. Colbeck, RNR, a veteran of the Newnes Expedition to Cape Adare. Tracing Scott's movements by the messages left there and at Cape Crozier, Lieut. Colbeck steered for McMurdo Strait. He reached it on 19 January to find that sixteen kilometres of fast-ice lay between *Morning* and Hut Point.

At first it proved impossible even to land the Expedition's mail. Between *Morning* and the still unbroken sea-ice lay three kilometres of turbulent half-rotted icefloes, which was dangerous to the ship and could have shattered a boat to splinters. Ice drifted out with the tide each day and when Scott returned to Hut Point the ships were sixteen kilometres apart.

A week later they were still eight kilometres apart, with less than a month remaining of the short sailing season. Scott began to plan a second winter.

Shackleton was still very weak, so he was invalided home and replaced by Sub-Lieut. Mulock, and the shore party was reduced by eight men, who were not replaced. *Morning* left for New Zealand on 3 March and *Discovery* was prepared to face the winter again.

This second winter passed as pleasantly as had the first, the main difference being that the ship was now brilliantly lit by acetylene gas instead of kerosene lamps. There were

debates and lectures, and the *South Polar Times* ran into
a second volume, in spite of the absence of Shackleton.
Scott made his plans for the summer journeys, but with a
nagging worry at the back of his mind that he might have
done the wrong thing in allowing the ship to be frozen in.

When he had done so he had assumed that it was normal
for the ice to go out from Hut Point every year. Now he
was not so sure – last summer might have been an exceptional one, and this one more normal. In which case
Discovery might remain in her frozen prison for many years
to come. So his travel plans were less ambitious for the
second season, since every possible man might be needed
to help free the ship.

The first journey of the new season was by Royds and Dr
Wilson to Cape Crozier, not to set the record straight but
for scientific reasons. Dr Wilson had found Royds's report
of the year before on the nesting habits of the Emperor
penguin almost unbelievable. The doctor knew that the
Emperor, one metre high and weighing up to thirty-six
kilos, was one of the most primitive birds, and a study of
the embryo might solve many puzzles concerning the
evolution of birds.

They found the eggs hatched and young birds running
about, which confirmed the fact that the eggs were
hatched in the winter. They found a few deserted eggs and
two chicks, which they took back to the base. The young
birds died because their keepers could not obtain the
proper food, while the eggs were infertile and contributed
nothing to the science of biology.

Scott planned three journeys for the second summer.
The Western Journey he would lead himself to the Victoria Land plateau, leaving Ferrar on the way to study

geology in two places where there was bare rock. Rock is
a rarity in Antarctica, and Armitage had named them
Cathedral Rocks and the Nunataks, the latter being an
Esquimau word describing a rocky island in a glacier.

Barne was to lead a journey to the south, travelling near
the coast and making a more accurate chart of its features
than Scott had been able to. Royds was to travel southeast
towards the centre of the Ice Shelf in an attempt to reach
the farther coast.

All the dogs had died on the Southern Journey, so these
treks were to be man-hauled from the first. This prospect
was welcomed by Scott, who set out on 9 September to lay
a depot for his Western Journey. He found an easier way
up the Ferrar Glacier, as it had been named, made a depot
under Cathedral Rocks and was back at Hut Point by
22 September.

Scott had reason to be satisfied with this trip. In five
days he had travelled a distance which had taken Armitage
three weeks, in spite of the fact he had endured very low
spring temperatures.

He started on the main journey on 12 October 1903,
taking four three-man teams and supplies for nine weeks.
Six days later they had reached Cathedral Rocks, 140 km
from Hut Point. But the metal-shod runners of the sledges
began to break up at this point and he had to return to
the ship.

Downhill and with the wind behind them they travelled
fast. The first eighty kilometres took only two days and
they had reached the sea-ice. The remaining fifty-nine
kilometres they did in *fourteen hours*, on foot and hauling
sledges.

These are amazing times and increased Scott's belief
in the power of human mind and muscle, for he wrote that

in his opinion such fast travel would be impossible using dogs. He set out again with fresh sledges on 26 October, picking up his stores and a third sound sledge on 1 November at Cathedral Rocks.

During their absence there had been a blizzard, which had blown an instrument case down the glacier and burst open the lid. The instruments were recovered, but a book of tables had been destroyed. Navigation without these special tables would be impossible, so that once out of sight of landmarks on the plateau they would again be steering 'by guess and by God'.

Scott held a council of war and it was decided not to return to base for another set of tables, since if they lost much more time there would be little remaining to make the journey. They would press on and rely on dead reckoning for finding their position. So on they went, but three days later they were halted by a blizzard and forced to lie-up in their tents for a week.

Putting themselves on half-rations, there was nothing to do but lie in the sleeping bags and wait for the weather to clear. It was daylight all through the twenty-four hours now, and after the first night sleeping was difficult. To pass the time, Scott began plotting a declination curve of the sun, to offset the loss of the navigation tables.

He had three fixed points to work on: he knew the position of the base, the date when the sun had first appeared after the winter, and the date when day and night are of equal length. He plotted his curve in the form of a graph, and when this was checked later on at the base it was found to be nowhere more than four minutes in error.

The weather cleared and Scott and Ferrar parted company, the latter to continue his geological work and Scott, with Seaman Evans and Stoker Lashly, continued towards the plateau. They had a strong head wind, but at an altitude of 2300 m they were suddenly in a flat calm, although they could still hear the gale roaring away lower down the pass.

On 13 November they were at 2700 m and had reached the featureless plain Armitage had described. Scott sketched and took bearings off the rocky peaks now low on the horizon behind them, and they stepped out into the unknown.

Altitude and the week of idleness in the tent had sapped their strength, and for two days they relayed the loads. They were on a rolling snow-covered plain, with low ridges seven or eight kilometres apart. At every crest they hoped to see something new beyond it, but always it was just another ridge.

They climbed the last of these ridges on 30 November then thankfully they turned back towards the coast, travelling faster now that the wind was behind them. They were short of food and fuel, and were eating cold lunches.

Near the head of the glacier the ice was badly crevassed, there were rifts in the surface metres wide and very deep, caused by the movement of the ice over the rocks below. Lashly had a bad attack of snowblindness, and the next day Scott and Evans fell through a thin crust of snow into a hidden crevasse, hanging by their sledge-harness over an icy chasm so deep they could not see the bottom.

After a struggle Scott was able to climb out with the aid of his own harness, and helped the still blinded Lashly to haul Evans out. Scott's dead reckoning did not fail them, and Lashly had recovered his sight by the time they reached the depot at the Nunataks.

They now had time in hand and provisions to spare, and

when they reached Cathedral Rocks Scott, for the only time in both his expeditions, declared a holiday. They made a standing camp and spent some days exploring the area, enjoying the sensation of walking without the drag of a sledge behind them.

The scenery around the camp was varied and there was plenty to enjoy. Here were the first streams of freshwater they had seen since leaving New Zealand and they were able to drink their fill. There was a fresh water lake, and even a bare patch of mud at the foot of the glacier.

They crossed the sea-ice to get back to the base on Christmas Eve, having travelled for eighty-one days and covered 1760 km. Scott wrote: 'We may claim to have made a most creditable journey under the hardest conditions . . . wherever my future wanderings may trend I hope they never lead me to the summit of Victoria Land!'

There were only four men aboard *Discovery* when Scott arrived. The others were at the ice-edge twenty-four kilometres north, beginning to saw a channel to the ship.

Scott spent a few days resting while he read the reports of Barne and Royds. Barne had charted the coast of Victoria Land as far as 80° south, while Royds had travelled 240 km to the southeast without sighting land. The question of whether Antarctica was one landmass or not was still undetermined.

A few days later Scott went to the camp on the edge of the sea-ice and decided that the attempt to saw a channel twenty-four kilometres long was useless. He decided to trust to nature to clear the strait of ice, and sent the men back to prepare for sea. With a small party, including Dr Wilson, he stayed to examine some tiny islands where there were rookeries of Adelie penguins nesting. They found that penguin eggs make splendid omelettes.

By the first week of 1904 it looked as if Scott's fears of the year before, that 1901–02 had been an exceptionally ice-free year, would be correct and *Discovery* might be frozen in for a third winter. He was beginning to plan for this when not one but two relief ships appeared, *Morning* and *Terra Nova*. They brought news that distressed Scott a great deal.

The Royal Navy had taken over the direction of the expedition from its civilian committee, and Colbeck had been promoted to commander and put in charge of both relief ships. He brought Scott very definite written orders. If *Discovery* could not be freed from the ice this season she was to be abandoned, and the entire expedition was to return to New Zealand in the relief ships.

Scott hated the thought of this, but orders are orders. If *Discovery* had to be abandoned there would almost certainly be a Court of Inquiry, which might mean a black mark against his name for the remainder of his service career. But he did not despair, there were still eight weeks of summer remaining before the ships must sail, and while he made plans for leaving her he was determined she should sail.

He began blasting a channel with high explosive, not for nothing had he qualified as a torpedo specialist, with only slow progress for three weeks. Then, during the last week in January, the ice began to break out from natural causes. A week later and *Discovery* could be felt stirring in her frozen cradle, and open water was only nine kilometres away.

The breakup stopped and Scott began blasting again, and blew up two kilometres of ice, then he had to stop because his blasting charges were running short. It looked

as if *Discovery* would have to be left after all, but on
14 February 1904 Scott's luck changed. A strong swell
developed and the ice began to drift out in huge floes. In
three days *Discovery* was free of the bonds that had held her
for two years, and the relief ships were anchored alongside.

Commander Scott wasted no time in leaving. Happy
working parties transferred the stores and fuel back into
Discovery, while the carpenters made and set up a large
cross in memory of Seaman Vince, the first Englishman
ever to die ashore in Antarctica. In spite of the sickness and
privation all the others had survived, and it can be said
that Vince did not die in vain. Because of his death Scott
had learned a great deal about how to travel and survive
in the land with the worst climate in the world.

Scott has told us that until Sir Clements Markham mentioned the *Discovery* Expedition he had no idea of becoming an explorer and spending nearly three years at the
bottom of the world in Antarctica. Yet he stands out as one
of the greatest polar explorers of all time, a reputation
founded on his work with the *Discovery* Expedition between
1901 and 1904.

He pioneered Antarctic travel, adapting the methods
of the Norwegian Fridtjof Nansen in the Arctic and adding
something of his own to fit them for the harder conditions
in the south. Before Scott no one had moved more than
a kilometre from their quarters. Scott showed how men
could travel hundreds of kilometres and live to tell the
tale.

He invented the depot and support party system for
increasing the range of the main party, and by using this
got nearer to the South Pole than any had done before. He
had not found a route to the Pole, but he had shown how

it could be travelled if one were ever found.

He had pioneered a new form of cold climate dress, with its light windproof outer garments and fur only for hands, feet and sleeping bags. Without windproofs it is doubtful whether the travellers could have hauled such sledge-loads, since fur garments would have iced up internally from perspiration and weighed much more.

Yet he was curiously blind about diet. Since the time of James Cook it was known that fresh food: fish, meat and especially vegetables, would prevent or cure scurvy. In the absence of these, concentrated lime juice was very valuable. At the base Scott had fresh seal or penguin meat available in practically unlimited quantities, but for the first year he made very little use of them.

He was prejudiced in the use of dogs for transport. As a young man he had been stationed in Canada, at Esquimalt in the west, during a time when there were Indian tribes there who not only used one breed of dog for hunting and transport, but another breed for meat. If Scott never saw dog-teams in use it is strange, but he must have heard of them, for they are used to this day. Also, he had met Fridtjof Nansen, and taken his advice about many things. Nansen was a great believer in dog transport and could have told Scott a lot about it.

Scott made a mistake in allowing the ship to be frozen in. He did not have to do it and no other explorer of the Heroic Age did so deliberately, although it sometimes happened by accident. The second involuntary season added little to the brilliant first year of the expedition.

Commander Scott was promoted to captain on his return to England, and decorated by the King. He was appointed a Commander of the Royal Victorian Order, and this could have been a disappointment to an ambitious man. Then, as now, it was usual to award the leader of a successful expedition a knighthood, and the expedition had been a success. Scott had discovered new land and pioneered with success a new form of travel.

Against this there is no doubt that he had put his ship to the hazard, since he did not have to let it be frozen in. The outbreak of scurvy could have been prevented, even with the knowledge available at the time. So Scott returned to the Navy and command of a battleship, while one of his companions of the Southern Journey took up the challenge of the South.

Shackleton

1908-1909

THE BRITISH ANTARCTIC EXPEDITION

1908–1909

Ernest Henry Shackleton

THE SHIP

Nimrod

Length	34 m	Engine	Two-cylinder compound
Beam	8.5 m	Power	82 kW
Draft	4.6 m	Speed	6.5 knots (12 km/h)

THE MEN

E. H. Shackleton*, C.V.O.
Leader
J. B. Adams *Second-in-command*
Sir P. Brocklehurst *Physicist*
Professor E. Davis *Geologist*
Dr A. F. Mackay *Surgeon*
G. E. Marston *Artist*
J. Murray *Biologist*

W. Roberts *Cook*
B. Armytage (*Ponies*)
B. Day *Electrician, Engineer*
E. Joyce* (*Dogs*)
Dr E. Marshall *Cartographer*
D. Mawson *Physicist*
R. Priestley *Geologist*
F. Wild* *Handyman*

* Veterans of *Discovery* Expedition

7

A Second Trip

ERNEST SHACKLETON was born in 1874 on a farm near Dublin in Ireland, the second child of a family of a brother and seven sisters. His father was a rather unusual farmer, since he had taken an arts degree from Dublin University.

When Ernest was four years old his father gave up farming and began to study medicine. He qualified as a doctor and migrated to England, setting up in practice at Sydenham near London, not far from the Crystal Palace.

At first Ernest was taught with his sisters by a governess, then went to a private school before attending Dulwich College. From the age of twelve he wished to go to sea, and when he was sixteen he was apprenticed as a deck officer in the Merchant Marine.

He joined *Hoghton Tower*, a full-rigged ship engaged in the nitrates trade with Chile in South America. During his four-year apprenticeship Shackleton made three voyages in *Hoghton Tower*, sailed round the world once and rounding Cape Horn five times. He qualified for his Mate's Certificate in 1894, then shipped as third officer in a tramp steamer.

Shackleton was anything but the bluff hearty seaman of fiction. He smoked, but he never drank alcohol, he liked poetry, especially Robert Browning, and he wrote very well himself. While still young he became a member of the Royal Geographical Society.

About this time he met Miss Emily Dorman, a friend of his sisters', and they became engaged. Shackleton left the tramp steamer and joined the Union Castle Line as Third Officer, becoming at the same time a Sub-Lieutenant in the Royal Naval Reserve. The Union Castle Line carried the mails to South Africa, regular voyages that gave more time at home for married men.

War broke out in South Africa in 1899 and Shackleton's ship, *Tintagel Castle*, was chartered to carry troops to Cape Town. With the assistance of the ship's surgeon Shackleton compiled a book, which they called *O.H.M.S.* This was published and sold at a profit, Shackleton making over his share of the royalties to a soldiers' charity. This gesture was to become typical of him, for he never wanted anything for himself.

He heard of the *Discovery* Expedition through the Geographical Society, and joined it in March 1900. He was already thinking of a career outside the Merchant Marine, and this may have seemed a way of making the break. He and Miss Dorman knew it meant more than a year of separation, but sailors and their womenfolk accepted such separations at that time. Shackleton sailed for the Antarctic in August 1901.

We have seen that after Scott's Southern Journey Shackleton was invalided home. His feelings were hurt at the time, but as it happened it was the best thing that could have happened to him.

He was young and good-looking, and on the voyage to England he quickly recovered from the scurvy. Unknown when he left home, he returned to find himself famous, one of three men who had set the 'Farthest South' record.

His contract to the *Discovery* Expedition expired in

September 1903, and he joined the staff of Sir George Newnes, the publisher who had sponsored the Cape Adare expedition in 1896. In January 1904 he was appointed secretary of the Royal Scottish Geographical Society, and he and Miss Dorman were married in April of that year.

In January 1905 he became the Liberal-Unionist candidate for Dundee, and resigned from the R.S.G.S. to become personal assistant to the head of a Clydeside engineering firm, Mr W. Beardmore. Here he did good work in recommending that the company begin making the newly invented diesel engines, but soon afterwards his political ambitions were dashed. He was defeated at the polls in a parliamentary election in 1906.

This marked a turning point in Shackleton's life. Had he been elected to Parliament he could have gone on to become a great statesman and industrialist. He was not ambitious for wealth or power, but he did want security for his family. He determined to seek this in a most hazardous way.

Antarctic exploration was still in men's minds, and many countries in Europe were fitting out expeditions to go there. Quite suddenly Shackleton made up his mind that he would lead a private expedition to the South, and do his utmost to reach the Pole. Such an achievement, he thought, could not fail to make him secure for life.

The British Antarctic Expedition (B.A.E.) was entirely Shackleton's private venture, sponsored by no learned society and with no Government promise of support. After it was launched the Australian and New Zealand Governments both gave contributions, but Shackleton did not depend on them for funds.

It cost £20,000 sterling (about $500,000 at present

values) which included the purchase of a ship. Shackleton raised most of this money himself, some as donations or loans on the security of a book and lecture tour to be produced on his return, some as gifts of equipment and supplies in return for advertising rights.

Mr Beardmore made a generous donation, and guaranteed a bank loan for more. By February 1907 Shackleton had enough money and equipment to be sure an expedition could leave England that year.

Shackleton was eager to be away, in case another expedition forestalled him. He had no wish to arrive in the Ross Sea to find others already there. A Belgian expedition failed to start, and a Frenchman, Professor Charcot, took his ship *Pourquoi Pas* to the Bellingshausen Sea, 3,200 km from Shackleton's proposed base.

Shackleton invited several of the *Discovery* team to join him, including Dr Wilson and Lieut. Barne, who could not go for various reasons, but he was joined by Joyce and Wild. In a published prospectus he said he intended to base the expedition near Hut Point and remain there with a shore party while the ship wintered in New Zealand waters before evacuating the base in the spring.

Soon after this was published a letter arrived from Captain Scott. In this he told Shackleton that he was planning an expedition himself, and asked him not to use McMurdo Strait as a base. This was a serious setback for Shackleton, for a condition for the loans of some of the money he had borrowed was that he would use McMurdo Strait and not hazard his ship by looking for a base in uncharted waters.

Since McMurdo Strait had been discovered and charted sixty-five years before Scott had no claim to any rights there, nor any legal claim to the buildings he had

Sea-washed berg with Mt Erebus in background (Scott 1910–1913) *Popperphoto*

ICE FORMS

The 'Castle Berg' (Scott 1910–1913) *Popperphoto*

Christmas Eve in the pack-ice (Scott 1910–1913) *Popperphoto*

erected. However, rather than quarrel with his old leader, Shackleton agreed to try and find a base in King Edward VII land, if his bankers would agree to the change of plan.

Because he knew the terrain around McMurdo Strait Shackleton had planned a shore party of only nine men. Feeling that this would be insufficient numbers in unknown country he increased his numbers to twelve, to allow for an extra supporting party.

He bought *Nimrod*, a wooden schooner with auxiliary steam, which had been employed in the sealing trade off the Labrador coast. She was cleaned and refitted on the Thames and rerigged as a barquentine.

Shackleton took only nine dogs, which increased to twenty-two during the expedition. These were more descendants of the Cape Adare expedition, and he collected them in New Zealand. From Armitage of *Discovery* he got the idea of using Siberian ponies for transport, which had been used in Spitzbergen with success.

Against the fact that all the pony food would have to be carried with them Shackleton saw that when each pony had done its work it could be converted into about forty kilos of meat which had cost nothing to transport to where it was needed. He also took a specially built Arrol-Johnston car, which was not a success, and a cinecamera which was. The film taken with this added a great deal of interest to his lecture tours when he returned to England.

He had already decided to increase the numbers of his shore party to twelve when he was awarded a grant of £6,000 from the Australian and New Zealand Governments; using this he increased his numbers to fifteen. This was a most fortunate decision, since the increase included Professor David and Douglas Mawson, who contributed greatly to the success of the B.A.E.

Shackleton was a more democratic leader than Scott, believing like Sir Francis Drake that the 'Gentlemen must hale and draw with the mariners'. Cook and handyman had the same treatment as the leader, shared the same quarters, wore similar clothing and ate the same food.

The only seamen in the shore party were Adams, known to Shackleton in his Merchant Navy days, with Joyce and Wild. It has been said that Shackleton selected men for mateship first and technical ability second. However he did it, he succeeded in picking out some first-class men on both counts.

Before leaving England *Nimrod* was inspected by the King and Queen at Cowes in August 1907. King Edward appointed Shackleton to be a Commander of the Royal Victorian Order, and Queen Alexandra gave him a silk flag to be carried on the journey to the Pole. While *Nimrod* sailed for New Zealand her owner remained in England on expedition business, travelling by mail-steamer to rejoin the expedition at Port Lyttelton early in December.

The Siberian ponies were in quarantine on an island in the harbour, where they were broken to harness and trained to draw a sledge. A steamship, *Koonya*, was chartered to tow *Nimrod* to the edge of the pack-ice, the object being to save both time and fuel. *Koonya*'s owners donated half the cost of this and the New Zealand Government paid the other half.

They had rough seas all the way to the pack-ice, and the strain of towing caused *Nimrod* to leak badly, so that the steampumps had to be assisted by the handpump. One pony was injured by the rough seas and had to be shot and thrown overboard.

They left Port Lyttelton on New Year's Day and

reached the pack-ice on 15 January 1908. Sheep carried in *Koonya* were slaughtered and passed across to *Nimrod*, to form the expedition's Sunday dinners for a year, and the tow was cast off. Already the B.A.E. had set one record, *Koonya* was the first steel ship to cross the Antarctic Circle, and now her wooden consort set her bows towards the Ross Sea.

Discovery had taken six days to steam through the pack-ice, but *Nimrod* took only two. By 17 January they were in the Ross Sea and steaming towards Edward VII Land. They sighted the Ice Shelf on 23 January and Shackleton steamed along its face to the west, looking for the inlets he had seen in 1902.

That year they had seen three inlets and charted them as fast-ice, that is ice firmly aground on the seabed. Shackleton thought that if he could find these again it would be safe to make a base on one of them, especially at the end of the summer thaw.

By doing so he would be keeping his word with Scott and not using McMurdo Strait as a base, and at this end of the Ice Shelf he would be 112 km nearer the Pole, which represented at least five days' travel, a very important consideration.

He found only the Bay of Whales still where it had been charted in 1902. The others, Barrier Inlet and Balloon Bight, were now features of some of the long icebergs adrift to the north. He took *Nimrod* into the Bay of Whales and was almost trapped inside by drifting ice. The ship was fortunate in escaping into the Ross Sea without being crushed.

Shackleton abandoned the idea of a camp on the fast-ice and steamed towards the coast of Edward VII Land.

Because of overcast weather he never even sighted it, and his course to the east was blocked by drifting ice.

There was a bare seven weeks of the sailing season left, and there were only two things Shackleton could do: he had either to break his agreement with Scott about wintering in McMurdo Strait, an agreement Scott had no right to suggest, or he could call off the expedition and return to New Zealand. Shackleton turned *Nimrod* towards McMurdo Strait.

At the beginning of February they were stopped by firm sea-ice twenty-four kilometres from Hut Point and Shackleton sent Adams, Wild and Joyce with a sledge and camping gear to have a look at it. We may imagine what this little journey meant to the *Discovery* men as the old landmarks came in sight. They found the hut in good condition, but the ice where *Discovery* had been frozen in had not moved since the winter after the ship left. Both 1901 and 1904 must have both been freak open years, and normally Hut Point remained icebound. Captain Scott had been luckier than he knew.

Shackleton made his base at Cape Royds, forty kilometres north of Hut Point. Its advantages were that it had splendid views of sea and mountains and was close to an Adelie penguin rookery, very convenient for omelette material in the laying season. Against this was the fact it was cut off from the Ice Shelf in high summer when the sea-ice went out.

They began unloading on 4 February, and had two serious mishaps. Another pony had to be shot and dumped over the side, and Mackintosh, a ship's officer who was to have been one of the shore party, lost an eye when he was struck by a cargo hook. The eight surviving ponies recovered quickly from their rough sea passage, and within two days were hauling loads across the ice. One slipped through a tidecrack into freezing slush, but its life was saved when a bottle of brandy was tipped down its throat.

In a week the framework of the hut was up, and all the stores were ashore except the coal for the stove and some of the instruments. While the men at Cape Royds got things shipshape ashore, Shackleton took the ship thirty-two kilometres to the south, to a place named Glacier Tongue, where he laid a depot of supplies for a journey to the Pole. Back at Cape Royds he found the sea-ice so broken and rotted that the remaining stores had to be landed by boat.

It was getting late in the season, and a sudden gale blew *Nimrod* out to sea. The men ashore built a shelter of bales · of pony fodder, while in the ship the seamen fought to free the ship of the ice from the frozen spray which threatened to capsize her. On 22 February there was a flat calm, and Shackleton called for a supreme effort by all hands to finish the unloading.

They worked for twenty hours without a stop. Thirty-six boatloads of coal were rowed through a kilometre of freezing slush, and the instruments and perishable stores were landed ashore. After hasty farewells *Nimrod* stood off to the north.

The shore party farewelled her with a cheer, then crawled into their sleeping bags to sleep the clock round. None of them had slept for more than three hours at a time for three weeks. Now sleep was the most important thing in their lives.

8

Antarctic Winter, 1908

CAPE ROYDS had a serious defect: there were outcrops of volcanic sand which poisoned small unprotected wounds. Four ponies swallowed some while licking it for the salt content, and died. This left only four of the ten shipped from New Zealand, and these were treated with the greatest care, carefully picketed out on fresh snow well away from the danger zone.

The hut measured eleven by five and a half metres, which would be considered too small for a family of four in developed countries, yet fifteen men contrived to live in it in harmony in spite of a winter lasting five months.

Apart from a stove and an acetylene gas plant, Shackleton took no furniture to the Antarctic. All his supplies were packed in cases made of plywood, then a comparatively new material, and furniture was made by the men as the cases were unpacked. The hut had seven two-man cubicles, a cabin for the leader, a kitchen and a darkroom. Two rooms were added just outside the door, one used as a store and the other as a biological laboratory.

A pony stable of fodder bales and plywood cases stood along one side of the hut, for since they had lost so many ponies there was no shortage of fodder. Earth was piled around the foundations of the hut and turned into ice concrete by pouring water over it. When frozen this sealed off draughts, and the hut was absolutely windproof.

Hut Point had been almost entirely shut in by cliffs, but at Cape Royds there were marvellous views. Mount Erebus was clearly seen, the vapour-plume from its active crater serving as an upper wind gauge for the meteorologist. Looking for a suitable object for a training run in camping methods for those new to Antarctica, Shackleton conceived the idea of having a party climb the volcano.

This was a good plan for it was breaking entirely new ground. Mount Erebus is one of the highest peaks of Antarctica, and the only known active volcano. It was only twenty-four kilometres from Cape Royds to the summit, so the party would never be far from help if they got into trouble, nor did it appear to be a difficult climb.

It was attempted by two three-man teams: a Summit Party (David, Mawson and Mackay) and a Supporting Party (Adams, Brocklehurst and Marshall). Only David and Mawson had climbed mountains before, but this had been in Australia or the tropics where the conditions are very different. The Summit Party had one-man sleeping bags which could be converted into rucksacks, the Supporting Party a three-man bag. They took one sledge, rations for ten days, and it was left to Adams to decide whether his party would also attempt the summit.

In two days they had done so well that they camped at 1750 m, and decided that both parties would attempt the summit. They dumped half the food, the sledge and the tentpoles to save weight, and camped in their sleeping bags with the fabric of the tent laid over them.

During the night a blizzard blew up, and next day the visibility was so bad they could not tell uphill from down. There was nothing to do but to remain in their camp until the weather cleared. During the day Brocklehurst had to go outside and was blown down the slope. Adams went to his assistance and was also blown downhill. Left on his own, Marshall could not control the big sleeping bag, which was blown inside-out. It took the party two hours to get back under cover, by which time they were all frostbitten.

The weather cleared next day and they continued the climb, although Brocklehurst's feet were still frostbitten. They camped on the rim of an old crater next day at 3480 m, but Brocklehurst could go no further. His comrades left him wrapped in all the sleeping bags and continued to the summit.

They found the height of Erebus to be 4080 m with a crater estimated to be about 275 m deep. They went down a little way over the edge, collecting samples of pumice, sulphur and feldspar crystals. Then they started back to camp, collected Brocklehurst and camped that night at 1700 m after recovering the sledge and tentpoles.

When it became known this climb created a stir in mountaineering circles, for a guideless climb with four beginners on an unknown volcano in Antarctica was unique. Only the state of poor Brocklehurst's feet marred the achievement. A big toe had to be amputated, and it was some weeks before he recovered from his experience.

Although the main object of Shackleton's expedition was geographic discovery he had recruited a fine scientific team. None were 'armchair explorers', all took to the trail during the summer.

As on the *Discovery* Expedition, meteorological readings were taken every two hours throughout the twenty-four. Adams looked after this project, servicing the instruments and taking readings from 8.00 a.m. to 8.00 p.m., when they were taken over by the night watchman.

The geologists made a mineral survey of Ross Island,

while Mawson studied glaciation and terrestrial magnetism. The biologist had fifteen fresh water ponds to explore,
and found primitive forms of life in them all. When the
sea-ice froze over he set fishtraps through the ice, the catch
from these going to the cook when science was finished
with them.

There was no idleness that winter of 1908. If a man had
little to do there was always a stack of plywood and improvements to be made to the dwelling.

The duties of messman and night watchman were
shared by all, including Shackleton but excluding the
cook. The messman brought in coal and ice to be melted
into water, chopped the seal meat, swept the floor, set the
table and did the washing-up. These were necessary
chores, but being messman was not a popular duty.

However, everyone enjoyed his turn as night watchman.
He took the meteorological readings, observed the be-
haviour of the Aurora Australis, the flickering curtains of
colour in the southern sky seen in these latitudes, recharged
the acetylene lighting generator, kept the stove going, had
a bath, washed his underwear, sewed on buttons and
darned his socks. Most men prepared an elaborate snack
for about 2.00 a.m., and any spare time in the ten-hour
duty was filled by reading or playing patience. In that
crowded hut the nightwatch was a chance to be alone for
a little, and solitude can be precious in such circumstances.

There was no formal programme of lectures or talks.
After the evening meal the men read, played cards or
chess, or listened to records. A small printing press had
been taken south and a book, *Aurora Australis*, was printed,
every member of the expedition making a contribution.
Two hundred copies were made, bound in plywood

polished with seal oil. These are now collectors' items and
any copy reaching the market brings a high price.

There were none of the tensions we sense in other expeditions during this southern winter of 1908 at Cape Royds,
and it passed quietly except for midwinter and birthday
celebrations. But the return of the sun was eagerly
awaited, for the men were keen to set out on their travels.

9

The Road to the Pole

By THE BEGINNING of August there were increasingly long hours of twilight each day. Shackleton decided to use this semi-daylight for depot laying journeys, to lift the supplies at Glacier Tongue south to Hut Point. The short journeys would make good training runs for the newcomers to Antarctica.

Shackleton led one party, Professor David a second which intended to travel towards the South Magnetic Pole, while Armytage was to cross the Ice Shelf towards Edward VII Land.

Shackleton left Cape Royds on 12 August and reached the *Discovery* hut next day. It was in good condition and well stocked with food, but a lot of snow had drifted inside. The party went on for two more days, reaching the Ice Shelf before being stopped by a blizzard. They retired to Hut Point and were weatherbound for five days.

Here they built a hut-within-a-hut out of food cases, with a false floor to prevent cold striking up from below. On 22 August they saw the sun for the first time since April and the blizzard blew itself out. Travelling light they returned to Cape Royds in one long march.

For the next few weeks there was a weekly convoy from Cape Royds to Hut Point via Glacier Tongue, a distance of thirty-five kilometres. On one journey Shackleton led a party which left Cape Royds, loaded up at Glacier

Tongue and reached Hut Point in one day, returning to Cape Royds in one long march the next. Shackleton's men began the season in much better training than had Scott's in 1902.

At the same time the ponies were being trained and exercised, and it was found that one pony could pull a sledge which normally required three men. But they could not use the horses as early in the year as the men or dogs, so Shackleton could not start his main Polar Journey until the end of October.

The car was not a success, which was not surprising in view of the primitive state of the automobile of the period. Shackleton was not upset by this because the car was only an experiment. He had too few dogs to make up many teams, so the four ponies comprised his main transport.

On 22 September Shackleton set out with two three-man teams to lay his first depot on the Ice Shelf. When they camped at Glacier Tongue they found they had been followed by three puppies. They were too young to face the expected conditions on the Ice Shelf, so they were left at Hut Point with a good supply of food and snow to lick for drinking purposes.

The conditions were worse than Shackleton expected on the Ice Shelf, and it was so cold that the kerosene froze in the primus stoves. On 6 October they built the depot, returning to Hut Point and a rapturous welcome from the pups.

Shackleton revised his plans. On 3 October Professor David left on his journey to the South Magnetic Pole, and because he would have to climb the Ferrar Glacier it had been decided in advance that his would be a man-hauled journey. With only four ponies left, Shackleton cancelled the journey towards Edward VII Land and Armytage was detailed to accompany David and lay a depot at the Nunataks, before going to examine the mudflats by Cathedral Rocks and complete the geological survey begun by the previous expedition.

Shackleton switched from three-man to four-man teams for his main journey, with a separate sleeping bag for each. Some felt that the three-man bag was warmer, but Shackleton thought that the privacy of the single bag was precious, especially during a long journey. Before he left he arranged that a depot should be laid at a place they had called Minna Bluff, and that a party should wait there to assist the Polar Party until 10 February 1909.

If the Polar Party had not returned by the time the ship had to leave, Murray was to ask for two volunteers and stay a second winter to search for the missing men the following spring. Shackleton made no secret that his object was to reach the Pole if he possibly could, and if he died on the way he wanted his experiences to be known to help those coming after him.

Polar Party

| Shackleton | Adams | Marshall | Wild |

Supporting Party

| Armytage | Brocklehurst | Joyce | Marston | Priestley |

The two parties left Cape Royds on 29 October and Hut Point on 3 November. Shackleton did not follow the coast, as Scott had done, but marched straight down the 168° line of east longitude. This way he avoided the crevassed surface where the glaciers flowing from the plateau of Victoria Land struck the surface of the Ice Shelf, and found the going much smoother.

He knew that the Ross and the Weddell Seas lay oppo-

site one another, and that both were bounded by a broad
Ice Shelf, so that there was the possibility of an ice-filled
strait separating two halves of Antarctica. If this were so,
then the Pole might lie in this strait and be relatively easy
to reach. And should he fail to reach the Pole, Shackleton
felt he might provide the answer to the question whether
Antarctica was one main landmass or not.

They had blizzards and soft snow at the start, and the
going was slow. Then the weather improved and they
advanced twenty-three kilometres on 9 November. Next
day the supporting party turned back.

Every few days they laid a depot, marked by a cairn of
ice blocks topped by a flag. By 21 November the loads
were so lightened that they no longer needed four ponies
for haulage so the weakest was slaughtered for food.

On 26 November they pitched camp three kilometres
to the south of Scott's record, and Shackleton had some
reason to be satisfied with his progress. Scott had reached
this point on 30 December with sick and hungry men, but
Shackleton was five weeks earlier and his men were fit and
vigorous. He could go a long way yet.

By 1 December two more ponies had been slaughtered
and deep crevasses were appearing in the surface of the
ice. Shackleton was sure they were approaching land, and
next day they saw mountains ahead as they neared the
southern shore of the Ross Sea. It seemed that there was
no strait through the centre of Antarctica to provide an
easy route to the Pole.

They camped for a day and climbed a small hill, Mount
Hope, to see if a pass lay through the mountain barrier.
Ahead lay a mighty glacier, its frozen slopes leading up-
wards into the blue distance. They named it the Beard-

more Glacier in honour of Shackleton's friend, and set out
to climb it on 4 December.

Shackleton was confident of reaching the Pole that day:
if the plateau at the head of the glacier was no higher than
Victoria Land; if they could get the pony to the top; if
they saved food by cutting one biscuit from the ration; if
they could average twenty-four kilometres a day . . . if . . .
if . . . if . . . .

Three days later the pony plunged through the snowlid
over a hidden crevasse and plunged to its death in the
frozen depths. This was a severe blow, for it meant the loss
of fourteen days' meat ration per man. Shackleton then
had to cut the food to make a week's ration last ten days.

To men hauling a sledge up a steep slope with a supercooled wind blowing into frostbitten faces, this was a tremendous sacrifice. It meant giving up one of their three
hot meals each day for the sake of being able to travel in
these bitter conditions for two extra weeks. They saved
sufficient to eat a full ration on Christmas Day, then cut
the ration back still further.

By 4 January 1909, Shackleton admitted that while
they might reach the Pole, if they did so they might not live
to return to the Base. They were at 3353 metres above sea-
level, and still climbing. He decided to continue three
more days, plant the Queen's silk flag, and then go back.

Two days later a blizzard held them up for three days,
and not until 9 January did Shackleton reach 88°23' south,
156 km from the Pole. They were now 3660 m above sea-
level and had discovered the highest plateau in the world.
But for the loss of the pony they might have reached the
Pole itself.

The cold and altitude made connected thought difficult, they were ravenously hungry and exhausted. Clumsily they planted the Queen's Flag and buried a brass capsule containing a record, then thankfully stumbled away to the north.

None of them were fit. They were scarred with frostbite, they had hunger-cramps and altitude headaches, and one after another had snow blindness. A little later, and they all were to suffer from dysentery. They had marched 960 km leading a pony most of the way. They had the same distance to go back, but now they had to haul a sledge as well.

They set off with two and a half days' rations to carry them to the first depot 224 km away, and they were to be a day and a half without food before they reached it. It contained only four days' food and in that time they had to descend a glacier that had taken almost three weeks to climb.

On their way up they had seen an outcrop they thought was coal, as important to industry then as oil is now, and decided to wait until the return before collecting samples. Risking death from hunger to do so, they collected them now, and coal it proved to be, showing that Antarctica had once had a tropical climate. But the four days' rations had to be spun out to last seven.

They reached the Ice Shelf once more, and were living now on a diet of half-cooked pony flesh, maize from the fodder and very thin pemmican hoosh. They talked of nothing else but food. They discussed memorable meals of the past and described what they would eat back at the base. They invented new dishes all of them very substantial. One of the favourites was Wild Roll, thought up by Seaman Frank Wild; it was composed of meat cooked with plenty of onions, then mashed to a paste. Spoonfuls of this were wrapped in rashers of the fattest possible bacon, which were laid on a slab of pastry which was then cut into slices and fried to a golden brown in deep fat.

It is not recorded whether any of these fantastic dishes was ever cooked, but it shows that the men who could dream up these dishes were living on a diet not only deficient in fats and starches, but also in protein and vitamins.

All were agreed on one thing, they wanted no jelly or trifle or any fancy food. Imagine wasting time eating such trash when you could have Wild Roll, or mashed canned salmon beaten up in thick porridge and served with melted butter.

At last they reached the depot they had made on 21 November, containing the meat of the first slaughtered pony. After eating some of it all suffered from dysentery and by 4 February they were too weak to march.

For the second time in six years Shackleton, a sick man, struggled over the Ice Shelf to safety. Only this time he was not the junior of the team, but the leader. He rallied the men and they struggled on, from depot to depot, becoming weaker and slower every day. On 23 February they reached the depot at Minna Bluff, and food in plenty, but there was no one there.

The men had waited until the tenth of the month, as Shackleton had instructed, then returned to the base. The Polar Party now rested for a day, eating all the time they were not sleeping, and nine days later marched into Cape Royds. They were so changed in appearance that only Wild could be recognized, because he was the shortest in the party.

10

The South Magnetic Pole

SHACKLETON'S JOURNEY was pure geographic exploration, in which the discovery of coal was an incident. Professor David's journey was wholly scientific.

The objects were twofold: to survey part of the coast of Victoria Land, and to reach the South Magnetic Pole. That a professor of fifty-one should be devoted to science is not unusual, but that he should be able to lead and survive such a journey is almost miraculous.

With Mawson and Mackay he left Cape Royds on 5 October, and took over a week to cross to Butter Point. This was near a penguin rookery, and had been named by the *Discovery* Expedition when cans of butter had been dumped there for the purpose of making omelettes in the laying season.

Travel was still safe on the sea-ice, so they decided to do the coastal survey first. This had been planned to extend 256 km north to the Drygalski Glacier Tongue, and *Nimrod* was to pick them up there in February 1909.

They had two sledges, and were relaying their loads from the beginning. Soon it was clear that they would have insufficient food to do both tasks. Dr Mackay had been experimenting with a blubber stove during the winter, and he now suggested they should live off the land during the coastal survey.

'There are seals and blubber', he said, 'and we can live

as the Greenland Esquimau does. With a blubber stove made from biscuit tins, the blubber for fuel and the meat for food.'

They agreed to give it a try. 'From then on', wrote Professor David, 'we ate as much seal meat as we could, with as little biscuit as possible.' It was a monotonous diet, its chief fault being its low fat content. In seals and penguins the fat is not blended with the muscular tissue as in animals of the temperate zone, but occurs as a layer of blubber between hide and flesh. Presently the frizzled strips of blubber from the stove became great delicacies.

For six weeks they lived in this way, arriving at the Glacier Tongue on 1 December. This was the biggest glacier outfall along the coast, which was why it has been chosen as a rendezvous with the ship.

They now had two months to devote to the journey to the South Magnetic Pole. After hunting for seals and cooking some of the meat to take with them, they made a depot of one sledge and the survey gear at a place they called Relief Inlet, where it was intended that they should meet the ship.

With one sledge and no need for relaying, they climbed the glacier to the plateau and an altitude of 2240 m. They found, as Scott had done above the Ferrar Glacier, that the land rose in a series of shallow waves.

On 16 January 1909 they reached the South Magnetic Pole (72°15′ south), though it would be more truthful to say that it reached them. The Magnetic Poles move in a figure-of-eight orbit, and on 15 January Mawson determined that if they camped where they were the Pole would reach them the next day. So they camped and took a continuous series of observations for twenty-four hours, and Mawson's prediction proved correct.

Now they were faced with the problem becoming familiar to every traveller in Antarctica during this Heroic Age – how to return to Relief Inlet on short rations in time to meet the ship.

It was 400 km distant and to reach it in time meant keeping to an average of about twenty-six kilometres each day. They managed to do this and by 20 January had made such good time they were able to increase the rations, and on only one day did they fall below their average. This was when Mawson slipped through the snow lid of a crevasse and hurt his leg, but even on that day they were only a few kilometres short of their aim. In the next three days they covered ninety kilometres and reached the depot they had planted at the head of the Drygalski Glacier.

On 1 February they were near Relief Inlet, but travelling slowly over rotting sea-ice and running short of food. They dumped the sledge and specimens gathered on the glacier and pushed on with minimum loads to the Inlet. They had been on the trail for four months and it was vital that they did not miss the ship. Arriving at Relief Inlet on 3 February they dug out the blubber stove, pitched the tent and settled down to wait.

Two dozed in the sleeping bags while the third kept watch for the ship and cooked a continuous snack on the stove. In the middle of the second day Mawson had just cooked a slab of penguin when he heard a gun.

'The ship!' he yelled, waking the others, 'the ship!', and he ran from the tent, to fall headlong down another crevasse. He was unhurt this time.

The sledge and geological specimens were recovered, and while they ate huge meals of civilized food they told the story of their journey. Including relaying, they had covered 2018 km, an average of eighteen kilometres each day. There had been neither depot laying nor supporting parties and the journey set a record for an unassisted sledge journey which stands to this day.

Nimrod picked up the rest of the expedition at Cape Royds and arrived in New Zealand on 24 March. Shackleton cabled the news of his arrival to England and found himself famous overnight.

In England he was knighted by the king, made a member of many learned societies and presented with decorations from foreign countries. Society hostesses competed with each other to have him as a guest at weekend house parties. Shackleton's gamble with the south had paid off in full.

His expedition had achieved more than any other, before or since. Using ponies for transport, he had found the southern shore of the Ross Sea and proved beyond reasonable doubt that Antarctica was one main landmass. He had found a route to the Pole, and discovered the highest plateau in the world. He had travelled to within 160 km of the Pole itself. The expedition had climbed Mount Erebus, charted the southern coast of Victoria Land, and reached the South Magnetic Pole. It had brought back scientific results and specimens of great value. And it had done all this with fifteen men in a forty-year-old wooden ship for less than £20,000.

Shackleton had a genius for leadership and picking good men, but it cannot be denied that he gambled with his own and their lives. His Polar Journey is an example. To reach the base he depended on a depot at Minna Bluff, which was not laid until he was on his way back. Had anything happened to prevent the depot being made, it would have been the death warrant for the men on that Polar Journey.

His arrangements for the relief of the Northern Party were even more inexact, for when he made them no one knew whether the Drygalski Ice Tongue could be reached on foot or not, and the same applies to the alternative meeting places further south. These terrific gambles were overlooked because of the success of the journeys.

Shackleton was criticized, but not for taking chances. What he was blamed for was using McMurdo Strait as a base, thus breaking his undertaking with Scott.

Scott had almost come to look upon the Strait as his own property, and Shackleton tried hard to respect this view. He had tried to find a base near the Bay of Whales, but decided it was too risky. If Shackleton thought this, then it was true at the time, for no one could accuse Shackleton of being afraid to take a risk.

Scott never accused Shackleton of breaking faith and there was no public disagreement, but they were never known to meet again, which was a pity. Scott could have learned a lot from Shackleton, and that generous man would have been pleased to pass on his experience.

Shackleton presented three problems to those who would follow and try to reach the South Pole: how to start earlier; how to travel faster; how to eat full rations all the way there and back. The man who found the answer to these questions would be the first to reach the Pole.

Amundsen

1910-1912

THE NORWEGIAN EXPEDITION

1910–1912

Roald Amundsen

THE SHIP

Fram, a three-masted schooner with auxiliary Diesel engine
First ship using oil fuel in Antarctica

Length 39 m		Draft 5.20 m	
Beam (on deck)	11 m	Beam (waterline)	10.40 m
Tonnage	392	Power	135 kW
Speed	4.5 knots (8.3 km/h)		
Diesel engine, 135 kW		Range 16,000 km	

THE MEN

Roald Amundsen *Leader*   Olaf Bjaaland *Carpenter*
Helmer Hanssen *Sailmaker*   Jorgen Stubberud *Carpenter*
Oscar Wisting *Sailmaker*   Henrik Lindstrom *Cook*
Knut Prestrud *Meteorologist*   Sverre Hassel *Cook's Mate*
              Hans Johanssen *Storekeeper*

There was no official second-in-command, but Hanssen
was usually regarded as Amundsen's deputy.

11

The Training

ROALD AMUNDSEN was born in 1872 on a farm near Oslo, the capital of Norway. They were a well-to-do family, and Roald's father owned a house in Oslo and a share in a shipping business as well as the farm. From an early age Roald determined to become an Arctic explorer.

He was sent to good schools, but was an indifferent pupil, and did his National Service in the Norwegian Army when he was eighteen. Then, doing as his mother wished, he attended the University, enrolled as a medical student.

He was still determined to be an explorer and to fit himself for this he lived as hard a life as he could. He slept with the window open and took a cold bath daily, no laughing matter where the winter temperature may drop to −40° C. He went on long foot or ski excursions in the middle of winter and on one of these excursions he nearly died. He was nineteen when he and a brother set out to cross Jotun Fell in winter, which had never been done before. The Fell is a plateau 2400 m high and 115 km across. They succeeded in crossing it, but could find no way down the escarpment because of ice and blizzards. They had to go all the way back.

They were twelve days on the summit, but had only food for three days with them, eking this out with some rancid rye flour they found in an empty herdsman's hut. They spent two nights there, spending the others lying in snowdrifts in their sleeping bags, and for the last three days they had no food at all. Good training for one who wished to explore the Arctic!

His mother died when Amundsen was twenty-one and he gave up the study of medicine. He then went to sea in the merchant service, intending to take a master's certificate to be able to command his own expedition ship when the time came.

Qualifying as First Officer, he signed on as mate of *Belgica* in August 1897, bound for the Antarctic. This was a Belgian Expedition led by a Captain de Gerlache, and Amundsen must have learned a great deal from his experiences, for everything went wrong.

De Gerlache had declared that the principal object of the expedition was a study of the South Magnetic Pole, but went instead to Graham Land on the opposite side of Antarctica. The ship was frozen in and drifted about with the pack-ice for thirteen months, Amundsen being one of the only two men on board who did not contract scurvy. The expedition accomplished nothing, returning to Europe in 1899. Two years later Amundsen qualified as a Master Mariner.

The part of the Arctic which fascinated Roald Amundsen was the North-West Passage, a sailing route around northern Canada from the Atlantic to the Pacific. Men had sought it since the sixteenth century and it was known to exist. Ships had probed from the east and from the west, some had got more than halfway through, but none had passed right across. It was Amundsen's ambition to be the first to do this.

In the same area as the North-West Passage is the North

Magnetic Pole, so that a voyage through one could be combined very well with research into the other. Amundsen's countryman Fridtjof Nansen, himself a great explorer, introduced the younger man to Professor Neumayer of Hamburg, an expert in terrestrial magnetism. With his assistance an expedition was formed and Amundsen sailed with six companions in *Gjoa*, a forty-seven-tonne fishing boat from Norway in June 1903. He stated he was intending to pass through the North-West Passage en route to San Francisco, and carry out magnetic research on the way.

The journey took three years, and during that time Amundsen became a master of Arctic travel. He learned from the Esquimaux how to live on seal and walrus meat, using blubber for fuel. While the ship was frozen into the ice he made long sledge journeys by dog-sled to the North Magnetic Pole, and became an efficient dog driver. He sailed the *Gjoa* through the North-West Passage, the first captain to do so, and was a famous man when he anchored in San Francisco in 1906.

Amundsen was also a good business man and had no trouble in raising funds for a second expedition. He now planned to sail right round the Arctic regions, from the Pacific back to the Pacific, with a side trip to the North Pole on the way.

This was an expedition that would appeal to the public, for though many attempts had been made to reach the North Pole, none had ever succeeded. Nansen had agreed to lend *Fram*, a ship specially built for one of his voyages, for this venture, when two items of news reached Norway almost at the same time. One was that the American Robert E. Peary had reached the North Pole on 6 April 1909, and the other was that Shackleton had reached the plateau of Antarctica and found a practical route to the South Pole.

Suddenly all public interest in the North Pole died away and with it the support Amundsen needed for his Arctic Circumnavigation Voyage. Amundsen thought the voyage would take four or five years, and the scientific results would be enormous. He had never cared greatly about reaching the North Pole, but it had been a necessary objective to gain public support and funds. Now he could not raise enough to set out.

However, he had a ship and funds enough to last two years, and then he had an idea. He would go to the South Pole. He reasoned that as Shackleton had been away only a year and a half, he should be able to reach the South Pole in that time, and if he did he would have no trouble raising more funds to finance an Arctic Drift expedition.

12

Framheim

FRAM sailed from Norway on 9 August 1910, and all except a few believed Amundsen was sailing for the Bering Strait to begin his Arctic Drift. He headed south, as was natural, since to gain the Pacific Ocean he would have to weather Cape Horn, as the Panama Canal was still under construction. Captain Scott had formed an expedition and sailed for the south two months earlier.

From Madeira Amundsen sent a short telegram to Scott: *Am going south – Amundsen.* Scott received this in Melbourne on 10 October 1910.

This created a storm of comment in English newspapers and the controversy has not quite died yet. Amundsen was accused of double-dealing and of taking advantage of Scott. We have seen how Scott regarded part of the Ross Sea almost as private property, and the feeling raised by Shackleton's going there. Actually the Ross Sea and its shores were frontier lands, open to any with the fortitude necessary to reach them.

However, Amundsen had no intention of going to McMurdo Strait. He had studied the accounts of *Discovery* and *Nimrod* expeditions, and concluded it would be possible to set up a base on the ice near the Bay of Whales. Shackleton had thought of doing this, but had not done so because of the changes in the geography between 1902 and 1908. Amundsen had a great deal of experience with ice conditions, and he thought the conditions of 1902 were freak ones and that the ice was normal in 1908. If it was still the same in 1911 he intended to make his base there.

Amundsen left one clear clue to his intentions before he sailed, he took with him 102 Greenland sledge-dogs. Had he really been going to the Bering Straits he need not have done this. He could have obtained good sledge-dogs in Canada or Alaska, and not had his ship cumbered with dogs all round Cape Horn and twice through the tropics.

Funchal in Madeira was Amundsen's last port of call before reaching the Ross Sea. He had almost to call at Cape Town for water, but rain at sea filled the tanks in time to prevent this. The men were on a water ration for a few days, but not the dogs.

Fram crossed the Antarctic Circle on 2 January 1911 and reached the pack-ice the same day. Four days later they were in open water and the Ross Sea echoed with the sound of a diesel for the first time. On 14 January they reached the Bay of Whales, open and free of drifting ice.

We now know that the ice in this area is fast-ice, securely anchored to the land. But this fact was not known until more than twenty years after Amundsen's visit, and his decision to make a base there was a brave one indeed.

A hut was assembled a few kilometres in from the ice-edge, and unloading began on 16 January. It was named *Framheim* ('Forward-Home'), and halfway to the ship a temporary *Dogheim* was established. There were now 116 dogs, for several litters of puppies had appeared during the passage south. Even during the unloading men began to hunt seal and penguins as food for themselves and the animals.

Amundsen was a great believer in holidays and one was declared the day after the ship arrived. Only essential work was ever done on Sundays, even when parties were on the trail.

On 4 February they were visited by Scott's ship, *Terra Nova*, but Scott was not on board and the ship was commanded by Lieutenant Pennell. Visits were exchanged between the parties and Amundsen went aboard *Terra Nova* for lunch. Pennell was seeking a place to land a second shore party, and the Scott-Amundsen controversy was not mentioned. Everyone was on the friendliest terms.

Fram was unloading the last of the stores when Amundsen left his base to lay his first depot. He intended to travel straight down the longitude of 163° east, laying a depot at each degree of longitude beginning at 80° south. His travel arrangements differed a great deal from those of Scott or Shackleton.

On this journey he took four men and three sledges, each sledge with a team of six dogs. On setting out the men wore fur clothing, but this proved too warm and was changed for windproof cloth.

Amundsen's men never hauled a sledge, except to start it from rest. One man, the 'Foregoer', went ahead to provide a mark for the dogs to follow, to break the trail, and to keep the direction. The men took turns at this and when not doing so either ran alongside the sledges on skis, if the going was suitable, or rode on the sledges themselves.

Greenland dogs in good condition can easily cover twenty-eight kilometres in a day and for the first three days out Amundsen made camp as soon as they had done this. On the fourth day, wishing to see what the dogs could do, he drove them a little harder covering forty kilometres between camps.

These long runs were partly possible because of Amundsen's arrangements for lunch. When an English party were on full rations they pitched a tent and cooked a lunch, which took about an hour and a half. Amundsen had with him some of the newly designed thermos flasks, which were filled with hot stew at breakfast time. Lunch could thus be eaten at any time, either riding on the sledge or sheltering in its lee while the men ate, at a saving in time, fuel and labour.

Eighty degrees south was reached on 14 February; here they unloaded the sledges, set up the depot and turned north again, then covering another fifty-five kilometres. In this one day they had travelled seventy-three kilometres and set up a depot into the bargain.

The depots were all built to the same plan, marked by a tall snow cairn topped with a black flag. From these a line of flags ran out north and south, east and west from the depot, each flag marked with its distance and direction to the centre. On the way back from 80° south Amundsen had a supply of dried cod – taken as food for the dogs – to spare, and he used the slabs of this stuck upright in the snow as route markers for later journeys.

Three more depot journeys were made before the winter, to 81°, 82°, and back to 80° south again. This last one arrived back in Framheim on 12 April, very late in the year for travel in the Antarctic. Only three dogs died, and the daily distance covered was very close to the ideal of twenty-eight kilometres.

Already Amundsen was working to a timetable. He reckoned he had been one day early arriving at the Bay of Whales, and three months later he was up to date. The base was established and three tonnes of stores were in depots towards the Pole, the most distant of these 384 km south of Framheim.

Amundsen felt he was in a good position. He was

Amundsen at the South Pole *Norsk Polarinstitutt*

Terra Nova in heavy ice (Scott 1910–1913) *Popperphoto*

SHIPS

Fram (Amundsen 1910–1912) *Norsk Polarinstitutt*

ninety-six kilometres closer to the Pole than any base in McMurdo Strait could be, and well stocked with seal and penguin meat. Scott hoped to reach the Pole – Amundsen knew that he could, and he also knew he could get there first.

The designer of Framheim was an Arctic veteran, Jorgen Stubberud. He had built it in Amundsen's garden in Norway, marked and numbered the sections, then struck it down to be reassembled at the Bay of Whales.

There was an entry porch and a kitchen, and one large room lined with bunks and lockers. There were nine men and ten bunks, the extra space being used to store instruments.

Each man had a bunk, a locker and a set of shelves. Nothing was allowed on the floor under the bunk except the boots the occupant had kicked off to get into it. The floor was polished and laid with rugs, the walls and ceiling painted, and the hut hung with pictures. Cooking and heating were by oilstoves, and it was lit by kerosene pressure lamps. It was a cheerful dwelling, very different from the rough-and-ready atmosphere of Shackleton's hut at Cape Royds.

The oil heater kept the temperature at about 20° C during the day, so that indoor work could be done in ordinary footwear and clothing. Amundsen had no need to sit with his feet in a haybox to keep them warm.

A storeroom outside the porch was built of empty packing cases and fitted with a door, and named the Penthouse. During the second depot journey there was only one man at Framheim, Lindstrom, and hut and penthouse were buried in snow during a blizzard.

Lindstrom could not clear the snow single-handed, so

he dug a sloping tunnel to the surface, which was later fitted with a trapdoor. He then had another idea, he dug a second tunnel at right angles to the first, sinking a deep pit at the end. He used this as a cesspit to get rid of the kitchen waste and slops. It was quite hygienic, for even hot water poured into it froze solid almost immediately.

When his mates returned tunnel digging became a popular sport. They dug a toilet tunnel, storerooms, a workshop and even a sauna bath. No Antarctic expedition had ever had such comfortable and well-equipped quarters as Framheim.

Dogheim was moved to Framheim after the ship left. The animals were housed in heavy canvas belltents set up in a deep pit with the excavated ice built up in a wall round about them. The poles were supported by a wall of ice, and as Amundsen said: 'The dogs soon cemented the poles firmly in without any help from us!' The dogs were fed on dried cod and seal meat, and fifty-five puppies were born during the winter.

Except for Lindstrom the cook, every man was responsible for the care and training of a group of dogs. On the depot laying journeys the sledges were found to be too heavily built, so during the winter Stubberud and Bjaaland rebuilt them, reducing the weight by eighteen kilos. The two-man tents of heavy silk were designed by Amundsen, and two of them could be set up end-to-end to give shelter to five. They were dome shaped, and so successful that similar tents have been used for polar or high altitude work ever since.

The expedition carried out little scientific work, for Amundsen never pretended that he had gone south for any other reason than to reach the Pole. However, a meteorological and magnetic record was kept, together with observations of the Aurora Australis.

There was no night watchman at Framheim. The reason why a night watch was kept on British expeditions was the danger of fire, which is always present in a wooden ship or hut heated by coalstoves. It is not practical in very cold climates to allow coalstoves to go out, for they take a long time to heat up again. But the oil-heaters at Framheim could be extinguished by turning off a tap, and heated up quickly next morning. So the last man to turn in turned the stove out, and since it was a chilly business there was keen competition not to be left to do it.

No weather readings were taken between 8.00 p.m. and 8.00 a.m., for as Amundsen wrote: 'I could see no point in doing this. The automatic instruments do the job very well, and they never get frostbitten!'

Including the leader, every man did a week's duty in turn as hut orderly, sweeping and polishing, setting the table and washing up. Saturday noon was the end of the working week, marked with a glass of hot toddy and a cigar after the evening meal. There were no lectures, and though they had a good gramophone and records it was never played except at weekends, or on birthdays or national holidays.

Sunday was a holiday for all, including the cook, and only essential work was done, the meals being provided by volunteers. For five months, from April until the end of August, nine men at Framheim lived well and happily, looking forward to the great journey to be made in the summer season.

13

The South Pole

ON 18 SEPTEMBER 1911 five men, driving five sledges drawn by ninety dogs set out from Framheim on a final depot journey to 80° south.

There were two reasons for taking such huge dog-teams. Amundsen knew that the going would be heavy in the early spring, and he wanted to select the best dogs for his main journey.

They were back at Framheim in nine days, and Amundsen made his final plans. He would take five men, with four sledges and fifty-two dogs. The men would either run on skis or ride on the sledges, travelling down the line of 163° east longitude. This would bring him 320 km to the east of the Beardmore Glacier, which he knew Scott planned to use, so he would seek a second pass to the polar plateau.

If he could not find one he could not reach the Pole. In that case he would bow out of the contest, having done his best, and go back to the Arctic. Amundsen was a realist in all things.

On the way to the yet unfound pass he would weed out the dog-teams, dumping the meat so obtained as food for the return, until at the head of the pass he would have three teams of six dogs each. Between there and the Pole he would reduce to two teams, again dumping the meat for food. The twelve surviving dogs would be brought back to Framheim and then to Norway, to live in the greatest of canine luxury for the rest of their lives.

He was not worried about time. Dogs could travel faster and start earlier than ponies, so that if he arrived at the Pole at all he would be ahead of Scott. He allowed three months for the polar journey, and *Fram* was due at the Bay of Whales in mid-January. If he set off in mid-October he should be back in time to meet the ship.

Roald Amundsen

Olaf Bjaaland   Sverre Hassel

Helmer Hanssen   Oscar Wisting

These were the five men who set out from Framheim for the South Pole on 19 October, and it was a very matter-of-fact departure. Lindstrom was busy baking bread and did not even come to the entry hatch to see them off.

They travelled light as far as 80° south, where all the supplies for the journey were already stored. This was just as well, for they passed over a badly crevassed area south of Framheim and Bjaaland had a narrow escape when he broke through the surface and fell. Eighty degrees south was reached in four days, an average of thirty-eight kilometres a day.

They stopped for a day to load up, while the dogs rested and were given all the seal meat they could eat. Now drawing full loads the speed was reduced to the planned twenty-eight kilometres daily.

Eighty-two degrees south was reached on 2 November, and the loads increased from the depot to the maximum again. They were now provisioned for ninety days with food either in depots behind them, packed on the sledges, or running on four feet drawing sledges. The dogs had now been reduced to forty-six.

Up to 82° south the route was already marked so from there on a cairn was set up every five kilometres to mark the return. The going was splendid, and south of 82° the day's march was lengthened to thirty-eight kilometres. They took regular rest days, the men reading in their sleeping bags while the dogs ate and slept.

Amundsen makes a polar journey seem almost as easy as a conducted tour to a beauty spot, while with Scott every step seems to be gained by superhuman effort. Yet country and conditions were similar for both and the reason for Amundsen's apparent easier time was that he was a professional explorer with greater experience, while Scott was a less experienced polar amateur.

This was most marked in Amundsen's use of dogs, giving him greater speed than Scott, also his men often rode on the sledges, especially as they ate their lunch from the thermos flasks. Amundsen's men could take a holiday from travel in fine weather, when running repairs could be made to their gear. The only respite from travel on Scott's journeys was when travel was impossible, and men could not leave the tents for more than a few minutes.

Yet Amundsen was no diehard traditionalist, when new methods were possible he would use them. He had a diesel engine in *Fram* and he used oil-heating at his base, and both were very new. When Amundsen had found a better way of polar travel than the dogteam he would use it. But he knew this time had not yet arrived.

Now his plan was to lay a depot for the return journey at every degree of latitude, and he laid the first of these at 83° south on 8 November. That same day they saw the first signs of land to the south, which were definite enough two days later to be charted as newly discovered mountains.

At the 84° Depot two of the new mountains were promi-
nent enough to be named Mount Nansen and Mount
Pedro Christopherson, the second in honour of a wealthy
Argentine businessman who was one of Amundsen's
supporters. A glacier hanging thousands of feet in the air
between the two mountains was named the Liv Glacier,
in honour of Nansen's daughter.

So far they could see no sign of a pass between the
mountains, for the Liv Glacier was too steep to form a
road. Still travelling fast, on 15 November they climbed
a ninety-two-metre ice-cliff and set up the 85° Depot
on top.

They were now on land, the first time any had set foot
on it since leaving Norway fifteen months before, and had
reached an altitude of 270 m. Amundsen declared a day
off while he thought things out, and with Hanssen and
Wisting climbed a hill south of the camp. He named this
for one of his sisters, Mount Betty, and from the summit
they saw a clear road to the south.

They were camped in a kind of glacial delta, the
branches of which stemmed from a glacier curving behind
Mount Nansen and rising steeply to the south. They
named this the Axel Heiberg Glacier, in honour of another
supporter, and from the crest of Mount Betty they were
able to map out a route through the broken country
towards it.

The forty-two dogs would all be needed to get their
loads to the summit, but once there they would be reduced
to sixteen. This was something Amundsen hated doing,
but he faced it as part of the price to be paid for attaining
the Pole. But it was hard to select one above another from
so many willing servants.

The climb began on 17 November, and next day the

Ice Shelf was out of sight. That evening they camped at 1200 m, and in most places such a rise in altitude would have meant a drop in temperature, instead the thermometer rose to 6° C and they marched sweating and stripped to the waist.

By 19 November they were at 1580 m, reaching a place where the Axel Heiberg was joined by an arm of the Liv Glacier. The surface was terribly broken and crevassed, and they had to cross from the east to the west side of the icefloe to find better going. Here they had to relay the loads for the only time on the entire journey. They made a temporary camp to rest the dogs while Amundsen, Hanssen and Wisting went forward on skis to reconnoitre.

Finding and marking a good track they drove on upwards with the sledges. They camped for the day at 3340 m on the summit of the plateau and with the glacier behind them.

This was a tremendous achievement. They had found, mapped and climbed a new route to the Polar Plateau in two days, with forty-two dogs and all on full rations. To climb no higher by way of the Beardmore had taken Shackleton twenty days, and part of that time his party were on short rations.

At this point, Slaughter Camp, they had the unpleasant task of shooting twenty-four of the dogs to provide food for the rest. As soon as they had done this they shifted camp to a fresh spot, Amundsen declaring a rest day for 21 November, but this was extended until 25 November when the party were held up for the first time by a blizzard.

For the next twelve days they moved over a surface so broken with crevasses they called it the Devil's Ballroom. Compared with the Beardmore the Axel Heiberg Glacier is short and steep and for a glacier it flows fast. Both are fed by the pressure of millions of tonnes of ice caused by snow-falls on the plateau, and as this ice flows down the glaciers it causes a disturbed area hundreds of square kilometres at the head of them. The Beardmore is much the longer and its slope is more gradual, but the disturbance at the source is less. Given equal conditions one route is probably as difficult as the other.

Since the blizzard it had been dull and overcast, with no sunsights to aid navigation, so Amundsen was travelling by 'dead reckoning'. After nine days the sky cleared and he was able to check his position and found he was right on course.

On 7 December they passed Shackleton's farthest south at 88°23′ south, and nothing short of complete disaster could prevent them reaching the Pole. They were travelling fast on full rations, and still had eighteen dogs.

They arrived at the South Pole on 14 December 1911, setting up a camp and calling it Polheim, staying three days. The Pole lay at the centre of the highest plateau in the world, a blizzard-swept wilderness of ice, 3360 m above sea level.

After twenty-four hours of continual solar observation the mean position of the Pole was determined and marked by a cairn with a sledge on top of it. A tent was pitched nearby, and in it were letters addressed to Captain Scott and King Haakon of Norway.

Amundsen was not being vainglorious in leaving a letter for Scott. He thought Scott would reach the Pole and he knew that there was a long and difficult journey ahead of him, and anything might happen. If anything did he knew Scott would tell of his achievement to the world, as he would, had the position been reversed.

The Pole was marked as he had marked his early depots, with four lines of flags at ninety degrees from each other and extending for ten kilometres in each direction. But there was one difference between the flags at the Pole and the depot flags – at the Pole each of the four lines of flags extended to the north.

The return march began on 18 December, with two sledges and eighteen dogs, the dogs being reduced to twelve between the Pole and the last depot. Amundsen was not squeamish about eating dog, looking upon it as fresh food and a good preventive of scurvy. He describes the taste as being like good beef, but maybe appetites on the summit of Antartica are not critical after living for ten weeks on preserved foods.

Across the Devil's Ballroom they were aided by strong tail winds, reaching the head of the Axel Heiberg on 4 January 1912. Two days later they were back on the Ice Shelf, suffering their only casualty on the way down when a dog was lost as it fell into a crevasse.

They were going strongly, and with the end of the journey in sight Amundsen increased his speed to forty kilometres a day, with a rest day after every five. Framheim was reached on 25 January, with five men, two sledges and eleven dogs.

Norwegians are not demonstrative folk, and Prestrud declares it was half an hour before they were asked if they had been to the Pole. *Fram* was in the Bay of Whales, and so was a Japanese expedition in *Kainan Maru*. The story of this expedition has never appeared in English, but we do know that the Japanese party did not spend the winter in Antarctica.

Only one other journey was made by the *Fram* expedition, when Prestrud, Johanssen and Stubberud took two sledges and fourteen dogs to Edward VII Land and were the first to set foot in it. But without depots or a supporting party they could not make a long journey, and were back at Framheim before the ship arrived.

The expedition left Antarctica on 30 January and reached Hobart early in March after a stormy passage. Here Amundsen met Douglas Mawson preparing to go to Adélie Land, and gave him all the surviving dogs except the eleven Polar veterans. These went back with *Fram* to Norway, where they lived happily ever after.

Amundsen's great journey was acclaimed all over the world, though in England admiration was tempered with anxiety about the fate of Scott. The Englishman was also in Antarctica making an attempt to reach the Pole, and nothing would be known of his fate for at least another year.

Roald Amundsen wrote a book and gave lectures about his journey, making enough money from them to invest in the family shipping business. During the First World War neutral shipping was a profitable business, and by 1916 Amundsen judged he had enough capital to build a ship for his North Polar Drift expedition.

This vessel he called *Maud* in honour of the Queen of Norway, who launched her with a block of ice instead of the usual bottle of wine. Amundsen sailed from Norway to begin his drift, a voyage which he thought would take four years.

While he was out of touch in the Arctic there was serious world monetary inflation, which swallowed up nearly all Amundsen's capital. He completed his voyage in 1921, but for the next three years he was heavily in debt. He had ideas of exploring the Arctic by air, but these ideas had to remain dreams until Lincoln Ellsworth, an American millionaire explorer, came to his assistance in 1924.

In 1925 Amundsen and Ellsworth made their first Arctic flights in a float-plane, and in 1926 Amundsen flew over the North Pole in an Italian-built airship, the *Norge*. The Italian designer and pilot of the ship, General Nobile, was a member of this expedition.

Nobile felt that insufficient credit had been given to Italy for the success of this expedition, although both the idea and the planning were the work of Amundsen and his Norwegian colleagues. An Italian expedition was formed and Nobile built another airship, the *Italia*, and took off from Spitzbergen in 1928 to fly across the North Pole to Alaska. The flight was a failure and the *Italia* came down among the pack-ice before getting to the Pole.

It was known that there were some survivors among the drifting ice, and in spite of his differences of opinion with General Nobile, Amundsen set out by air to search for them. He left Tromso in Norway on 18 June 1928, and after a few routine radio messages from the aircraft there was silence. Amundsen was never seen again.

Scott

1910-1913

THE BRITISH ANTARCTIC EXPEDITION

1910–1913

Robert Falcon Scott

THE SHIP

Terra Nova

Length 57 m	Beam 9.50 m
Draft 5.80 m	Tonnage 392
Engines Steam compound	Power 105 kW

Maximum speed under steam 6.5 knots (12 km/h)

THE MEN

Officers

Captain R. F. Scott, C.V.O., RN *Leader*
Lieut. E. (Teddy) Evans, RN *Second-in-command*
Lieut. V. Campbell†, RN

Capt. L. Oates (*Ponies*)
E. Atkinson, RN *Surgeon*
Lieut. H. Bowers, RIM (*Supply*)
G. Levick†, RN *Surgeon*

Scientific Staff

Dr E. Wilson* *Zoologist*
T. Griffith-Taylor *Geologist*
F. Debenham *Geologist*
R. Priestley*† *Geologist*
G. Meares (*Dogs*)
A. Cherry-Garrard *Zoologist*
Dr G. Simpson *Meteorologist*

E. Nelson *Biologist*
C. Wright *Physicist*
H. Ponting *Photographer*
B. Day* *Engineer*
Trygve Gran, R. Nor. Navy (*Skis*)

Lower Deck

W. Lashly*
T. Clissold *Cook*
R. Forde
T. Williamson
G. Abbott†
H. Dickason†
Anton Omelchenko *Groom*

W. Archer *Steward*
E. (Taff) Evans*
T. Crean*
P. Keohane
F. Browning†
F. Hooper *Steward*
Dmitri Gerof *Dog-handler*

* Veterans of previous expeditions
† Members of Northern Party

14

The Preparation

FROM SEPTEMBER 1904 until January 1906 Scott was busy lecturing and writing a book about the voyage of *Discovery*. After a short spell in Admiralty he went on to command battleships – *Victorious* in August 1906, and *Albemarle* in January 1907.

He had one nasty incident in the latter, when she was rammed by *Commonwealth* during night exercises in the Atlantic. No lives were lost, however, and the damage was slight. The Court of Enquiry exonerated both captains, saying that there was no fault in the handling of either ship. Night exercises were essential in the war training of a fleet, and the risk of collision must be accepted as part of the price of efficiency.

As a result of publishing his book Scott had met people in artistic and literary circles, and became friendly with James Barrie, the author of *Peter Pan*. Through him he met Kathleen Bruce, a sculptor aged 26, thirteen years younger than Scott.

Soon after the *Albemarle-Commonwealth* incident they became engaged, and Scott's letters to her have been published. They make curious reading, an odd mixture of love letter and financial statement. Ever since his father's bankruptcy Scott had worried about financial security, although as a captain in the Navy and the author of a successful book he was quite well off.

He kept in touch with many of his shipmates of *Discovery* days, and another expedition was being vaguely discussed. This never reached the serious planning stage and had Shackleton reached the Pole it is doubtful if it would ever have done so.

Scott and Kathleen Bruce were married in September 1908, and in January 1909 Mrs Scott wrote to her husband that she was pregnant. Scott was delighted with this news, for he had a strong family sense. But in his reply to this letter Scott mentions something that may have set him thinking about leading another expedition to the south. He tells her of a dinner party with his admiral, at which two of his fellow guests were Captain and Mrs David Beatty.

No officer of any Navy in this century had such a brilliant career as Admiral of the Fleet Lord Beatty. 'I knew him as a lieutenant', Scott wrote to his wife. 'He has slipped into two wars, and will be an admiral at thirty-eight.'

To do this Beatty had been lucky, for there had been no naval wars of note since the time of Nelson early in the last century. But between 1896 and 1898 there had been a war against the Dervish empire in the Sudan, and Lieut. Beatty had been appointed second-in-command of a flotilla of gunboats on the Nile. These were shipped out in sections and assembled and launched above the Cataracts, where there is nearly 1280 km of navigable river.

They were in action twice, both times against forts guarding the river, once at a place called Dongola and once at the battle of Omdurman. Beatty was in command both times, the first because his senior officer had not arrived, and the second because the same senior officer was in hospital ashore sick with fever. For his successful

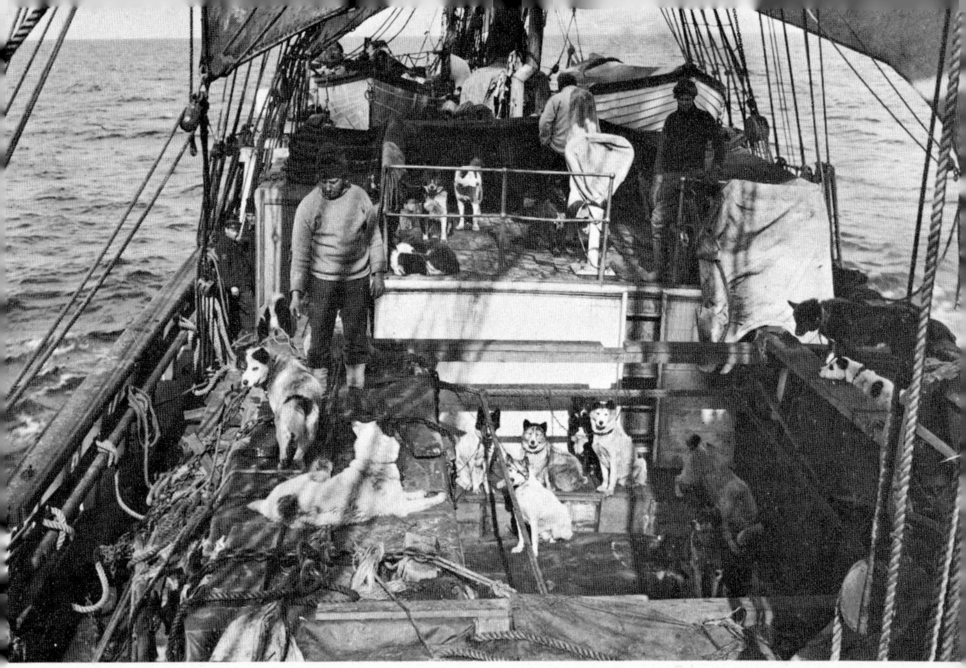

On the deck of *Terra Nova* (Scott 1910–1913) *Popperphoto*

CRAMPED CONDITIONS

Winter quarters (Scott 1910–1913) *Popperphoto*

Scott's winter quarters by moonlight
(Scott 1910–1913) *Popperphoto*

ANTARCTIC CAMPS

Camp at One Ton Depot (Scott 1910–
1913) *Popperphoto*

Camping on the ice halfway up the
Beardmore Glacier (Scott 1910–1913)
Popperphoto

first action he was awarded the D.S.O. and for the second he was awarded a bar to this – that is, he was awarded it a second time – and promoted to the rank of commander. He was then only 28.

, Beatty was four years younger than was usual for a newly promoted commander, and it was difficult to fit him into the structure of the navy at the time. He was sent to China, as naval attaché to the British Ambassador at Peking. He had not taken up this post when the Boxer Rebellion broke out, and the foreign legations at Peking were besieged. Beatty formed and led a naval battalion to the relief of the legations, to be awarded further decorations and gain promotion to captain. He was then only twenty-nine and was the youngest to be so promoted since Lord Nelson.

Now he had been a captain for nine years, and the dinner party was to celebrate his approaching promotion to admiral, for a captain is always advised a few months beforehand of this important step in his career. The occasion must have made Scott think very hard about his own naval future. It is customary in that service that when an officer is promoted to admiral all those who were senior to him as captains are retired on the same day, so that a captain never serves under a senior officer who was once junior to him. Scott would be very much aware of this.

He was three years older than Beatty, and four years junior to him as a captain, so the question of premature retirement did not yet arise. Maybe it never would, for there was open talk about war in the near future with Germany, and the navy was being expanded as never before in peacetime. But the government might change and naval expansion might be halted if the opposition gained power.

Somehow, Scott had to gain the next step in rank within four years, before a captain of his own seniority was promoted over his head. He could think of only one way to do this and gain a knighthood at the same time. He would form a new expedition, and be the first man to reach the South Pole.

So he organized the largest expedition to leave Europe during the Heroic Age, and its purpose was declared to be purely scientific. However, no one doubted that one of its main objects was to reach the South Pole, although Scott had played down this side of the expedition both in his lectures and articles in the press. But he knew that in the public's eye no number of scientific papers or specimens would excuse a failure to reach the Pole.

Scott was still convinced of the superiority of man-hauled sledges over other forms of polar transport, but he had been impressed by Shackleton's use of ponies. In view of Shackleton's great losses in getting his ponies to Cape Royds they can only be regarded as a limited success, and they were never employed in the Antarctic after this present expedition.

Both Amundsen and the American Peary had made famous dog journeys in the Arctic, but as we have seen Scott appeared to be prejudiced against the use of dogs. The numbers he took with him had little effect on the expedition either way. But he thought mechanical transport had a future, so he took three tractors with caterpillar treads, the forerunners of the bulldozers and tanks of today. These were tested on a glacier in Norway where the tests were witnessed by Fridtjof Nansen.

'What do you think of them, Dr Nansen?' Scott is reported to have asked. 'Would you take them south?'

Dr Nansen shook his head. 'Myself, I would take dogs,

and dogs, and still more dogs!' he answered. 'If a dog
breaks down, it provides food for other dogs – even for
men. But if a motor breaks down, what is it? Just a heap of
oily metal in the snow.'

Scott had been elected a member of the Royal Yacht
Squadron, and *Terra Nova* was registered as his private
yacht. As a member of the Squadron Scott was entitled to
sail under the White Ensign, just as if his ship were a unit
of the Royal Navy. Also, as a yacht, *Terra Nova* was not
subject to the Board of Trade loading regulations and the
Plimsoll marks, which indicate the maximum depth a
merchant vessel may be loaded with safety, were painted
out.

The ship sailed from Cardiff in June 1910, with members of the expedition scattered over half the world. Scott
was still in England on expedition business before leaving
by mail-ship for Cape Town joining his ship there,
while Wilson and the expedition's secretary went by mail-
ship to Melbourne to buy stores and engage more members of the staff. Meares was in Siberia buying dogs and
ponies, while seamen were being signed on in New
Zealand to work the ship back to Port Lyttelton after she
had landed the shore parties in Antarctica.

Scott received Amundsen's famous cable in Melbourne
in mid-October 1910. There is no record of his reactions
at the time, but just before setting out for the Pole a year
later the wrote to his wife:

I don't know what to think of Amundsen's chances . . . and . . . I have
decided to act exactly as I should have done had he not existed. Any
attempt to race must have wrecked my plan, besides which it doesn't
appear to be the sort of thing one is out for . . . it is the work that
counts, not the applause. Don't worry . . . that this matter troubles
me. To be quite honest, I very rarely think of it.

Terra Nova sailed from New Zealand on 25 November, much earlier than any previous expedition. Scott had planned two shore parties, a long way apart, so as to get a good base line for the magnetic research, and he needed extra time for this. Here he was to be disappointed. All the evidence showed that the later a ship entered the pack in December the quicker her passage through it. Scott was to find that he gained practically nothing by making an early start.

Like all the coalburning expedition ships of the period, *Terra Nova* burned a great deal of fuel, so before leaving Port Lyttelton she took on as much as she could carry. She was overloaded and badly stowed, as a result of Scott's haste to be on his way. Her holds were crammed, her decks cluttered and her accommodation overcrowded. Extra deckhouses had been added as laboratories and storage space, and she had a hundred tons of deck cargo: coal, petrol, kerosene, lubricating oil, four ponies, pony fodder, sledgedogs and three motor sledges stowed on top of the deckhouses. Lieut. Evans wrote in his Journal, 'She's like a Noah's Ark stinking of kerosene and black with coal!' Had she been sailing as a merchant ship the Plimsoll mark would have been well under water and she would not have been allowed to leave port.

Scott was very fortunate not to lose the ship. In the early hours of 2 December the engineer reported that the steam bilge pump was choked, and that the water was flooding into the engine room. The watch on deck manned the hand pump, but soon that too was choked. The crew and most of the scientists were then organized into two watches to bail out the ship with buckets through the engine room skylights, working two hours on and two off.

Work as they would the water gained on them. She was

leaking through both the side and the deck seams, and the lower she settled the faster she leaked. The situation was desperate when Lieutenants Evans and Bowers, with the engineer and the shipwright, began to cut a way through a bulkhead to get at and clear the suction-boxes of the pumps.

The ship rolled under sail on the swells of the Southern Ocean, for the water had risen so high in the engine room that the fires under the boilers had been put out. It was after ten o'clock that night before the way through the bulkhead was clear, and Evans and Bowers stripped and dived into the hot and filthy bilge water to clear the suction-boxes of the pumps.

They knew the ship could fill and sink under them with little warning as they worked in the dark; water over their heads, tons of cargo stowed above and around them, and no chance of escape if the ship took a sudden plunge. It took six hours to remove twenty pailfuls of tarry sludge, a mixture of coal dust and engine oil washed down from the deck cargo, and not until four in the morning was the hand pump cleared. It choked several times through the morning, and was not fully reliable until noon the following day.

Bailing out with pails could then stop, but the weary men still had twelve hours' toil at the hand pumps. Just before midnight the boilers were flashed up again and steam applied to the bilge pumps. Only then could the ship be considered reasonably safe, after forty-eight hours' work for all hands. They had lost two ponies and one dog by drowning, and twenty tons of oil, coal and petrol had been jettisoned to lighten the ship.

Terra Nova entered the pack on 9 December, taking nearly

three weeks to force a way through, and Scott was only one week earlier into the Ross Sea than he had been in 1902, at the cost of sixteen days' consumption of coal. By 3 January they were off Cape Crozier and through the telescope they could see their old message post.

Dr Wilson was eager for the base to be made here, so that the breeding habits of the Emperor penguins could be studied through the winter. However, rough seas prevented a landing, so they bore away for McMurdo Strait.

Arriving there the next day, Scott decided to set up the base at Cape Evans, halfway between Cape Royds and Glacier Tongue. Because of the sea-ice they could only get to within two kilometres of this point, but the ship was able to lie right alongside the ice and unloading commenced at once.

At this season there was daylight right through the twenty-four hours, and the shore-party worked from seven in the morning until midnight, with short breaks for meals, while the ship's company worked watch and watch, four hours on and four off. This unequal division of labour was a great strain on the shore-party.

By 6 January 1911, Meares had two dog-teams at work, and two days later Oates had some ponies in harness. One motor sledge was lost when the ice-edge crumbled and dropped it into the sea, but the other two showed great promise as they hauled loads from ship to shore over the level sea-ice.

On 21 January all seemed well. The hut was up and almost ready for occupation, and most of the stores were ashore. The sea-ice had broken further out and the ship was only 360 m from the base. Four days later Scott set out on a depot laying journey, seventeen days before Amundsen had set off on his first trek to 80° south. The Norwegian was still unloading, but was so far in advance of his schedule he had declared a holiday for all hands.

The Depot Journey
Scott

Atkinson	Crean	Gran	Oates
Bowers	Teddy Evans	Keohand	Wilson
Cherry-Garrard	Forde	Meares	Dmitri

Eight ponies Two dog-teams

None of the men were fresh. For three weeks they had worked seventeen hours a day every day, with snatched meals and insufficient sleep. Bowers had not slept for seventy-two hours before he set out and was working until the last minute, handing over as Stores Officer to a deputy. In addition he had been kicked by a pony just before the start, and he had Cherry-Garrard put a dressing on the wound in case the doctor declared him unfit and would not let him go.

By 29 January they reached the Ice Shelf, thirty-eight kilometres from the base but they had covered 145 kilometres to get there, relaying loads and making many diversions over rough sea-ice. Near the edge of the Ice Shelf they dumped some pony fodder calling the place Safety Camp.

The snow was deep, the ponies floundering in it up to their bellies. Captain Oates had devised some pony snow-shoes, but had only time to train one pony to use them. They were such a success that Scott decided to camp and train all the ponies, sending two men back to bring up the spare sets which had been left at the base.

They could not do this because the sea-ice had gone out and they were now cut off from Cape Evans, except for a long and dangerous overland journey, until the sea froze over again in the winter. Scott had to go on without the pony snowshoes, with the ponies floundering up to their bellies all the way.

Dr Atkinson went sick with a poisoned foot which made it impossible for him to travel, so he was left in a tent at Safety Camp with a supply of food, to be picked up on the way back. On 2 February the depot party left the camp and started south.

On 12 February they arrived at Minna Bluff, having been held up for three days by a blizzard, and set up a depot eighty-six kilometres from Cape Evans. Two of the ponies were failing and the horse expert, Captain Oates, suggested they be slaughtered and used as dog food. Scott did not take this advice, and instead sent the three weakest ponies back to Safety Camp in the care of Evans, Forde and Keohane. It took them fourteen days to reach camp and only one pony survived the journey.

The party was now seven men, five ponies and two dog-teams. They were short of dog food and one team became so ravenous it attacked and almost killed a pony before being beaten off.

Scott had planned the main depot to be at 80° south, but found he could not get so far except at the risk of wrecking his transport and the lives of his men. The depot was made at 79°27′ south on 16 February, sixty-seven kilo-metres short of his target, and named One Ton, from the amount stored there.

One thing was clearly proved by this journey, dogs and ponies could not be used together as transport. They do not travel at the same pace, and to try and keep them together on the trail frustrates the dogs and exhausts the ponies. For the return journey Scott went ahead with the dogs while Oates followed with the ponies.

Oates reached Safety Camp on 26 February, having been on half-rations for five days, and found Scott waiting for him. Scott had travelled fast, although one team had broken through the lid of a crevasse and he had climbed twenty metres down a rope to rescue them.

Meanwhile, Dr Atkinson had recovered and made a solitary journey to the old *Discovery* base at Hut Point. Lieut. Pennell had been there from the ship, after visiting the Bay of Whales and seeing Amundsen. In a letter left for Scott he said he had not tried to land Campbell in King Edward VII Land, since their presence might have clashed with Amundsen's Party, but intended to put them ashore near Cape Adare on his way back to New Zealand.

When Scott read of Amundsen being at the Bay of Whales he wrote:

We must go on as if this had not happened . . . and do our best for the honour of our country, without fear or panic . . . Amundsen's plan is a very serious menace to ours. He has a shorter distance to the Pole by sixty miles . . . I never thought he could have got so many dogs to the ice . . . his plan of running them seems excellent . . . and . . . he can start earlier in the season, an impossible condition with ponies.

At Safety Camp they lived in tents with the ponies in the open, summer was over and winter on its way. There is little of spring or autumn in Antarctica, and it was important to get under shelter as soon as possible, and the only shelter within reach until the sea froze was Hut Point.

There were two ways to get there, both dangerous. They could either travel over the rocky coast of Ross Island, or along the fringe of rotten sea-ice on the shore.

Scott dismissed the overland route at once. It was where Vince had been killed in 1902, and it would be impossible for the ponies. But the approaching winter was already cementing the old ice along the coast with new, but this was still weak and brittle.

On 28 February Bowers, Cherry-Garrard and Crean set off with five ponies for Hut Point. The sledges carried food for several weeks because it would take time for the new sea-ice to become a safe road to Cape Evans.

Soon after the start a pony collapsed and died, so they restowed the sledge and carried on with four. Utterly exhausted, they camped that night on a solid-looking floe; during the night this broke away from the land and began drifting out to sea. They awoke to find themselves on separate ice-rafts, but by daybreak they and the four ponies were all together again on one large floe.

Next day they were attacked by killer whales, who are carnivorous and live on seals. These reared their heads over the edge of the floe trying to upset it and spill the party into the sea.

Crean managed to get on to a smaller floe and used a ski to paddle it ashore, then set off to get help from the others at Safety Camp. Six hours later he returned, and first the men and then the sledges were hauled ashore, together with one pony.

Then the tide turned and the floe began drifting seaward again. There was nothing to be done about the three ponies still on the ice but to shoot them and leave them to the killer whales.

A week later the party reached Hut Point, and camped in the old building for six weeks before they could reach the base at Cape Evans in April. Of the eight ponies that had left in January only two survived.

The results of this depot journey cannot have been cheering for Scott. They had covered 480 km, not a long way by Scott's own standards, but a fine effort by men exhausted by a dangerous sea passage and three weeks' ceaseless toil before starting out. The expedition's transport plans were in jeopardy, with nearly half the ponies dead and little to show for it. One Ton Depot had been set up far short of his objective, and his second party was ashore 960 km from where he had planned it and in a different direction. Meanwhile, Amundsen was at least four days' journey nearer the Pole than himself, and did not have to worry over the state of the sea-ice.

Scott had been reared in an era of intense national pride, when men were supposed to be able to do almost anything, given the will. Scott had the will, and so had many of his comrades. The ponies had proved a partial failure, and he had too few dogs to take a leaf out of Amundsen's book. He had two tractors but he was not hoping for a great deal from them.

He had men. They would reach the Pole, aided by ponies and dogs. But the last stages of the journey there would be done by men alone, hauling their own supplies.

The Hut at Cape Evans was a pleasant place, built on a shelving beach and sheltered from the blizzards by a rocky ridge. It was double-skinned and floored, the spaces between filled by an insulation made of dried seaweed. There was a porch serving as a storeroom and a stable along one side, both built of empty packing cases.

The two rooms were divided into an outer galley and living-space for the men, the inner the officers' mess. Scott had a small cabin, and so had Ponting, which was also his darkroom. The building was lit by acetylene gas.

As in Scott's first expedition, the fiction that it was a

Royal Naval shore establishment was preserved. Lieut. Evans was the naval chief of staff and Dr Wilson his scientific counterpart. No scientist ever approached Scott direct with a query, and some never spoke to him at all.

There is some evidence that Scott and Ponting, the photographer, did not quite hit it off together. Ponting was a splendid photographer and had contracted to go south for a year, write his own book, but share his photographs with Scott. Apart from taking pictures he took no part in the work of the expedition.

The hut was heated by coal, so there was the usual night watch shared by the officers except Scott and Ponting. Meteorological readings were taken by Simpson during the day and the watchman at night. There was plenty of work: rations to pack, ponies and dogs to exercise and train, sledges, clothing and trail gear to make, repair, or modify.

They had a good library, a gramophone with a large selection of records, and lectures on all manner of subjects three nights a week.

15

The Worst Journey in the World

PERHAPS THE MOST readable book about the *Terra Nova* Expedition was that written by Apsley Cherry-Garrard under the above title. This title refers not to the depot or the polar journeys, but a trek to Cape Crozier on a fantastic bird-nesting expedition.

During the *Discovery* expedition evidence was found suggesting that Emperor penguins incubated their eggs in the open air during the middle of winter on the barren peninsula of Cape Crozier. Dr Wilson, a keen ornithologist, was anxious to learn more about this and had wished that the expedition base could have been set up on the Cape. When this was proved to be impossible he determined to make a winter journey to Cape Crozier, set up a camp and collect eggs at different stages of incubation.

There is no daylight during midwinter, so the journey would have to be done in moonlight or darkness. It would have to be man-hauled, for neither dogs nor ponies could have faced the conditions. The three men who set off were Dr Wilson, Lieut. 'Birdie' Bowers and Cherry-Garrard.

There are many incidents to illustrate the almost insane devotion to science by members of this expedition, but this journey is the most extreme. There may have been worse journeys made by men under duress, but as a voluntary effort by men free to make a choice, Cherry-Garrard's description will stand.

They set out in the pitch darkness of midmorning on 27 June, and spent the next night in the old building at Hut Point. They had six weeks' food on two small sledges, toggled one behind the other, and hoped to haul these both at once. This was a vain hope and they were forced to relay the sledges.

The journey itself was used for research into food values. They took only pemmican, biscuit and butter, with milkless and sugarless tea to drink. The same *weight* of food was eaten by all, but the quantities of the three items varied. Today it is difficult to see the point of such an experiment.

At first the route ran across a bay called Windless Bight. Some days the temperature was almost as high as zero with an excellent sledging surface, but with a fifty-knot wind blowing straight in their faces. On other days there was dead calm, an unshaded candle would burn steadily in the open air, the temperature would be down to $-50°$ C and exhaled breath crackled with a sound like crumpling tinfoil as it froze. But the snow would have a surface like rough gravel and the sledges would not slide. Under both of these conditions the sledges had to be relayed.

The 107 km journey took nineteen days, and everything they possessed, clothes, tent, sleeping bags and sledges, was caked in an armour of ice. They only slept in short snatches in the icy sleeping bags so they were tired all the time. They cheered themselves up with talk of the snug igloo they would build of snow-blocks at Cape Crozier, and of the penguin egg omelettes they would cook.

They reached Cape Crozier on 19 July, and looked for material to build the igloo but there was no snow. The Cape was swept by almost continuous easterly gales and the surface was bare rock. The best they could do was a rock grotto, roofed with the sledges and a strip of canvas.

The tent was pitched in front of this to act as a porch.

They observed that the Emperors did hatch their young in winter, watching as both parent birds took turns in sitting on the egg which they supported on their down-covered feet and covering it with a feathery flap of skin. Five eggs were collected, and three reached England safely.

Day had made a blubber stove for them, which at Cape Evans had worked well with seal blubber for fuel but when used with penguin blubber at Cape Crozier spluttered badly. Dr Wilson was splashed by burning oil in the left eye, and was in such pain they had to use morphia from the medical kit. For a while it was feared he might lose the sight of the eye, but he recovered.

Then a blizzard swept the Cape, wrecked the grotto and blew away tent, sledges and cooker. This amounted to a sentence of death, a penalty for taking the power of the winter too lightly. They lay huddled in their sleeping bags until the blizzard eased, then they ate a cold meal which each thought would be his last. During a blizzard the temperature rose, and when it dropped again they expected to freeze to death without the tent and hot food.

Then their luck turned. The sky cleared for the first time since leaving the base and there was an almost full moon. By its light they found a sledge, the tent and the cooker, none of them badly damaged. They did not find the blubber stove, though one wonders whether they looked for it very hard, so there was no longer any possibility of staying at Cape Crozier. They set out on the return journey straight away, travelling much faster with lighter loads and any wind that there was behind them. They reached Hut Point in six days and Cape Evans the day after.

There are many unanswered questions about this mad journey. Since Scott must have agreed to it, why was there not a supporting party to assist over the first stages and another at Hut Point to assist them on their return? Or why was a party not sent to the Cape in the autumn, to make a depot for use later on? Around this time there is evidence of Scott being absent minded.

When Cherry-Garrard, the sole survivor of the 'Worst Journey', returned to England in 1913 he made an appointment at the Natural History Museum in South Kensington to deliver the three surviving Emperor penguin eggs.

He was passed from official to official until he reached the Chief Ornithologist, who was deep in conversation with a visiting V.I.P. The following conversation took place.

Cherry-Garrard: 'I have brought three Emperor penguin eggs from Cape Crozier to present to the Museum.'

Chief Ornithologist: 'Indeed! Please put them down over there.'

Cherry-Garrard does so and waits.

Chief Ornithologist: 'There's no need to wait – I'm sure they will be quite all right.'

Cherry-Garrard: 'I should rather like a receipt, please.'

Chief Ornithologist: 'Oh, there's no need for that! They'll be quite all right, I'm sure.'

Cherry-Garrard: 'I should still like a receipt!'

And eventually after several hours and interviews with more officials, he got one.

Some months later he visited the Museum with Captain Scott's sister, and in spite of the receipt the curators denied there were any such things as Emperor penguin eggs in London.

16

Scott — The South Pole

AS THE SLEDGING SEASON drew near Scott seems to have dismissed the Polar Journey from his mind. In the autumn he had failed to set One Ton Depot as far south as he had planned, but he did not use the spring to advance it further. Instead he set out as one of a man-hauling team to lay a depot on the Ferrar Glacier to aid a party who were to make a geological survey of the Western Mountains.

He was away from Cape Evans for two weeks, to begin again on preparations for the Polar Journey on his return. A field telephone had been laid to Hut Point, and for a few weeks the road between these places became the busiest highway Antarctica had ever seen.

Amundsen depended on depots with no supporting parties, but Scott had only one depot. He relied heavily on supporting parties, and he planned to have four four-man parties at Mount Hope near the foot of the Beardmore Glacier. Each party would be self-contained, but with interchangeable personnel. Tractors, dogs and ponies would be used as far as Mount Hope, but from there on the expedition would be man-hauled.

One supporting party would return from Mount Hope, and three would begin the ascent of the Beardmore. About halfway up another party would turn back. Somewhere after that the final selection for the Polar Party would be made. Four men would return while the others went on.

Everything was designed to suit four-man parties. The sledges were to be pulled by four, the tents to sleep four, the cookers for four, and rations packed in four-man weekly units. Each man had his own single sleeping bag.

The parties were drawn from the following personnel:

Scott	Lt. Evans	Dmitri	Crean
Atkinson	Day	Wilson	Mearnes
Bowers	Lashly	Keohane	Oates
Cherry-Garrard	Hooper	P.O. Evans	Wright

with ten ponies and twenty-two dogs

Scott thought that the most difficult part of the journey would be getting to Mount Hope. Once they were free of caring for transport animals, and man-hauling their loads, he thought the journey would be almost pleasant. There were ten ponies, two tractors and two eleven-dog teams, but only three ponies and the dog-teams could be considered really fit. The tractors had done well over short distances while unloading the ship, but had not been tested over longer runs.

Lieut. Evans, with Day, Lashly and Hooper, left Hut Point with the tractors on 24 October 1911. Their instructions were to run to 81°30′ and wait there for the main party. Scott watched them claw their way up onto the Ice Shelf, the first mechanical vehicles to do so, and they were then going well.

They broke down beyond repair only sixty-four kilometres from Hut Point, when the lubrication system failed, not being able to withstand long runs at low temperatures. So there they lay, in Nansen's words, 'just a heap of metal in the snow!'

Evans dumped a load of pony fodder to be collected by

Scott, and with his team set to man-hauling half a tonne of man rations to the rendezvous. They arrived there on 15 November and laid Mount Hooper Depot, named after Hooper who spent his spare time raising an enormous snow cairn over it.

With the first party under Lieut. Evans already out on the trail, Scott and the remainder left Hut Point on 1 and 2 November. Scott found the wreckage of the tractors and was disappointed but not surprised. He picked up the fodder dumped by Lieut. Evans and pushed on.

The going was soft and the ponies repeatedly broke through the icy crust, dragging the sledges down with them. After lying up one day because of a blizzard they reached One Ton on 15 November.

(On the same day Amundsen made his depot at 85° south and climbed Mount Betty to seek a pass through the mountains.)

They were a day at One Ton making up the loads, then the depot was rebuilt and marked on top with a red kerosene can. At this point Scott calculated that to get to the Pole and back he would need to average twenty-four kilometres each day, which was worrying. So far he had only averaged two-thirds of this distance.

However he had no trouble in keeping up his average over the next sixteen days, by which time he reached Mount Hooper. On 24 November the first supporting party returned: Day and Hooper, two men instead of four. Scott has given us no reason why he changed his four-man party system at this point, but it was odd that he did, especially as neither of these men could navigate.

Slaughtering ponies and leaving depots at intervals, they reached the foot of the Beardmore Glacier where they slaughtered the last of the ponies on 10 December. Next day the dogs went with the main party a short way up the glacier, until Scott decided he did not need their assistance and sent a second two-man party back, Meares and Dmitri. On the trail there were now:

Atkinson	Crean	Keohane	Scott
Bowers	Lt. Evans	Lashly	Wilson
Cherry-Garrard	P.O. Evans	Oates	Wright

with three sledges, all man-hauled.

On 11 December Scott's journal is cheerful. The ponies had done better than he had expected, and were now out of their misery. The dog-teams had done better still, and were now safely on their way home. There were twelve fit and determined men, and everything depended on the human spirit.

We have seen that Scott had a mystical faith in the capacity of man-hauled transport, a conviction that moral strength can overcome physical failings. As it can, to a point, and Scott was soon to find what that point was.

(On 11 December Amundsen was far away on the plateau, three days' march from the Pole.)

During the first part of the climb up the Beardmore Scott thought things were not going too badly. He was five days behind Shackleton's time in 1908, having been held up by blizzards on the way to Mount Hope, but his supplies were in better shape and his party was stronger. Nor were they having to relay, so every step forward was a step in the right direction.

This tempered optimism shows in a note sent back with Meares. 'Things are not so rosy as they might be, but we keep our spirits up and say the luck must turn . . . I can keep up with the rest as well as of old.'

Scott was conscious of the fact that at forty-three he was the oldest man in the party, and making the statement that he was not too old for the task.

Things were only just going well. The way was steep, the surfaces dragged, and the wind was in their faces. But they could travel every day, and only over the worst places did they have to relay a sledge. But by 16 December they were six days behind Shackleton's schedule and Scott was worried. Things improved, and five days later he had caught up three days.

Here another party turned back: Atkinson, Cherry-Garrard, Keohane and Wright. The following continued on:

Bowers	P.O. Evans	Lashly	Scott
Crean	Lt. Evans (Teddy)	Oates	Wilson

Scott had stopped trying to keep to a daily average and now worked on a time basis. They man-hauled for nine hours a day, which, added to the time spent making and breaking camp, meant fifteen daily hours of work seven days a week. They only rested when they were held up by weather.

They were becoming very hungry, but Christmas was a bright day. They hauled as usual, but ate double rations finishing off with Christmas pudding, preserved ginger and a tot of brandy. On 27 December one sledge was towing worse than the other and they decided to lighten it by dumping four sets of skis, taking on another set for the use of the Polar Party if the surface should improve. It is clear that at this point Scott intended the final party to consist of four men.

The members of the final team had not yet been chosen, and at one time when he was suffering from indigestion he had doubted if he could be one of them. This had now cleared up and he resolved to lead the party himself. He felt he had to have a second navigator, which could be only Bowers or Teddy (Lieut.) Evans. Bowers, being stronger physically, was Scott's choice for the Polar Party.

This was a sound choice, but the same cannot be said for Scott's inclusion of Dr Wilson. He was a slightly built man of thirty-nine, not physically strong and had a medical history of T.B. He had qualified in medicine but had not practised for years, and had gone with the expedition as a zoologist. He and Scott has been close friends since the *Discovery* Expedition, and the choice of Wilson seems to have been a sentimental one.

Logically the fourth member of the team should have been the strongest man of the party, who was probably Lashly. Scott wanted a seaman for fourth man, since he did not want it said it was an all-officer party. He knew Evans better than Lashly, and Evans was his choice.

Apart from Wilson that made it an all-navy team. Captain Oates was army and had done amazingly good work with a poor lot of ponies. Without the ponies they would certainly not be so far on their way. The report would look much better if there was an army man in the final party. Scott could not make up his mind who to drop in favour of Oates, then he scrapped the four-man idea, taking five to the Pole and sending three back from the polar plateau on 4 January. Teddy Evans, Lashly and Crean went off to Cape Evans. Food was beginning to run short and the going was difficult, but Scott thought he had a good chance of getting to the Pole.

(That same day Amundsen started to descend the Axel Heiberg Glacier, travelling with two dog-teams. On 6 January 1912 he was back on the Ross Ice Shelf.)

Through the records of this expedition runs a recurrent theme that the return of a supporting party was going to be one long picnic. After all, the route was marked and there were no depots to build. Except possibly for Day and Hooper, who arrived back at Cape Evans three days before Christmas, no one had a pleasure trip.

Meares had a difficult journey, made no easier for lack of a common language between himself and his trail fellow Dmitri. Meares could not navigate, and the trail markers had been levelled by a blizzard early in December. He had trouble finding the depots, and had it not been for the dog-teams both men would probably have died. But they did not have to use their strength man-hauling, and had energy to spare to restore the trail markers. They are probably the only party to ever celebrate two Christmas Days during the same journey, since Dmitri's Russian Christmas fell on a different day to Meares's English one. They arrived at Cape Evans on 4 January 1912.

Dr Atkinson's party started from halfway up the Beardmore three days before Christmas, and before leaving they presented the others with Christmas gifts; half a scarf, an ounce of tobacco, a pair of socks, things that mean a lot among friends in this situation. Cherry-Garrard dismisses their 878 km journey in less than one page of his book, but it was a tremendous effort. In fact, it was a far greater journey than Scott's farthest south effort in 1902.

They got into a badly crevassed area going down the Beardmore, and Keohane broke through the crust eight times in half an hour. They collected geological specimens near a mountain Shackleton had named Cloudmaker. They encountered thick weather, near starvation and dysentery. They all had symptoms of scurvy, and were pretty far gone when they lurched into Cape Evans on 26 January 1912.

Teddy Evans's party had the worst time of all, with farther to go and the need for three men to pull a sledge designed to be pulled by four. Food was not a weight factor in any return journey, since they only carried enough to get them from one depot to the next. But in the case of Teddy Evans's party this meant splitting open the ration packs and taking three-quarters of each. Being the men they were they probably took a little less than their due, so that they were always short in their ration.

Over the first half of their 965 km journey they made good time, with a sail rigged on the sledge and a tail wind to speed them on. In the third week of January Teddy Evans had signs of scurvy, but it did not seem to be serious and cleared up in a few days.

The scurvy symptoms reappeared at the end of the month, by which time they were short of food and there was a mysterious shortage of kerosene in the depots. They had to cut down on cooking, and Evans weakened so fast it appeared he might die before reaching Cape Evans. While he was still strong enough to stand the others would strap on his skis and tow him behind the sledge. But by 13 February he became too weak to do this, so he was toggled into his sleeping bag and towed on the sledge.

Lashly and Crean were far from fit themselves, though Crean was the less affected of the two. After five days of towing the sick man they could go no further. In writing, Evans ordered them to leave him in his sleeping bag and go to save their own lives. They refused to obey.

So Lashly remained with Evans while Crean set off to walk the last fifty-six kilometres to Hut Point for help. He had to cover the whole distance on cold food and without rest. He could carry no camping gear and there was the danger that if he sat down he would freeze and die.

Crean covered the distance in thirty hours of continuous marching, and found Dr Atkinson with Dmitri and a dog-team at Hut Point. *Terra Nova* had arrived and had brought down a supply of fresh onions. Onions are one of the best cures for scurvy, so some were put on the sledge.

Evans was still alive when they reached the camp, but Dr Atkinson did not think he could have lived another day. Luckily scurvy responds quickly to rest and the right foods and soon Evans was strong enough to travel, wrapped in his sleeping bag and strapped to the sledge. Rescuers and rescued reached Hut Point on 22 February 1912.

Teddy Evans became famous as Evans of the *Broke*, when he was the hero of an action against German warships in the Channel during World War One. He later commanded the Australian Fleet, and as Admiral Lord Mountevans was in charge of all fire brigade and rescue work in London during the Second World War, 1939–45. Lashly and Crean were both decorated with the Albert Medal for 'Saving life and for their steadfastness and courage during their terrible journey.'

The five men who reached the Pole were Bowers, P.O. Evans, Oates, Scott and Wilson.

Before the parties separated on 4 January 1912 the sledges were shortened and the runners repaired. While doing this P.O. Evans cut his hand, but did not report the injury in case he missed the chance of going on with the Polar Party.

He had to report it on 7 January, as the injury had gone septic and he could not use his hand. It was treated by Wilson, but little could be done for such an injury in the days before antibiotics. That same day Scott wrote in his Journal: 'Cooking for five takes half an hour a day longer than cooking for four . . . something I had not thought about.' This was because the cookers were designed to cook four servings and when used for five had to be done in two stages.

The next day they passed Shackleton's Farthest South, and here a note of doubt begins to creep into Scott's Journal, not that they would not reach the Pole, but that they might not get back. All but Bowers were feeling the cold badly, and Evans's hand was getting worse. They could not afford to be held up for even a day.

They made a last depot forty-eight kilometres from the Pole, with four days' food to get them back the ninety-six kilometres to the previous one. This was cutting things fine and Scott was aware of it. Things were getting desperate.

On 16 January Bowers saw a cairn ahead. There was a line of marker flags, the footprints of men, and the tracks of many dogs. They had reached the Pole, only to find Amundsen had forestalled them by five weeks.

(On that same day Amundsen was within seven days' travel of Framheim, well fed and travelling fast behind two vigorous dog-teams.)

17

Return from the Pole

THEY WERE two days at the Pole, taking photographs and fixing its position anew. Scott placed the actual Pole a few hundred yards away from where Amundsen had done, but there was no doubt as to who was the first arrival. The discrepancy might have been due to a small fault in the explorers' instruments, and both could be equally right.

'All the daydreams must go!' Scott wrote in his Journal when he found Amundsen had arrived at the Pole, summing up the spirit of the party as they began the return journey. The hopeful spirit at the top of the Beardmore Glacier gave way to something like despair.

Yet Scott had not failed, or disgraced himself in any way. He writes about 'our poor slighted flag', which is very close to self-pity. He had done what he set out to do, and no one could detract from that achievement. He had lost nothing, for he had said he did not intend to make a race for the Pole. But he was sick and weary and not thinking very clearly.

They began the return on 18 January, with the wind at their backs for the first time in weeks, and covered thirty-two kilometres a day with a sail rigged on the sledge. This easier travel must have been welcome to Bowers, for it was his skis which had been dumped before the last supporting party left them, and for some days he had trudged knee-deep in snow while the others slid along easily in their skis.

Two things were worrying Scott at this time, the weather and Evans's health. It was just past midsummer, but the weather was breaking up. Meanwhile, Evans was weakening all the time, his hand did not heal and he became frostbitten very easily. He had been a tower of strength from Cape Evans to the Plateau, but since injuring his hand he had rarely been able to pull his weight.

There was no light relief in the day's work these days, no expedition jokes or songs on the march. There was just nine hours' hard slogging work each day, with one disability after another recorded in the Journals. By themselves some of these were serious enough, but taken together they began to spell disaster!

28 JANUARY 1912. Marched 22 miles. Evans, five fingers blistered by frostbite. Oates, big toe turning blue-black.

30 JANUARY. Marched 19 miles. Wilson strained tendon in leg.

31 JANUARY. Marched 15 miles. Evans lost two fingernails. More of Oates toes going black.

2 FEBRUARY. Marched 17 miles. Scott fell, badly bruised shoulder.

5 FEBRUARY. Marched 18 miles. Evans lost three fingernails, nose beginning to suppurate.

Yet in spite of their ailments they were making good marches. One reason was the tail winds and another may have been the drop in altitude. Since leaving the Pole they had only descended about 300 m., but at least the going was downhill and the air became denser as they went on.

They reached the head of the Beardmore Glacier on 7 February and picked up three and a half days' rations to get them to the Cloudmaker. This is the mountain halfway along the Beardmore Glacier near where Shackleton had found a seam of coal. Here Scott gives himself and Bowers a clean bill of health, mentions that Wilson's leg is improving, reports that Oates feels the cold badly, but is only seriously concerned about Evans. From this may be deduced that either Scott could not see what bad shape the party was in, or he was refusing to admit it to himself.

The three and a half days' food had to last for six as they traversed the badly crevassed area that had held up the supporting parties. Finally they reached the Cloudmaker depot, picking up four days' food and some geological specimens.

The drop in altitude had made no improvement in Evans's condition, though it had slowed up his decline. His hands and face were covered with suppurating frostbites, all his finger and toenails had gone and his speech was affected. On 17 February he collapsed in a coma on the march and died a few hours later.

They were grieved at his death, yet there is a note of thankfulness in the Journal entries that his sufferings were at an end. Dr Wilson wrote that death was due to a fall on the plateau, but it seems clear that the doctor was refusing to look facts in the face.

It seems more likely that Evans died of scurvy. At this same time his namesake almost died of this disease, and both had been eating similar food and doing similar work under the same conditions. There can also be little doubt that the four survivors of the Polar Party were also affected by this deficiency disease.

Scott read the funeral service over Evans, who was buried in his sleeping bag under a cairn of ice blocks. That same afternoon they reached the Ice Shelf, and the tail wind died away to a flat calm. That put an end to the daily thirty-two-kilometre marches of the past few weeks.

Only very rarely now did they cover more than sixteen kilometres in the day. Yet they had no doubts about reaching the base, and talked of what they would do when they arrived.

On 24 February came a fresh blow. At the Southern Barrier Depot there had been a mysterious shortage of kerosene, which was not serious if they could make better time. Here, for the first time in his Journal, Scott begins to wonder whether they will be able to make Cape Evans.

A week later at the Mid-Barrier Depot the oil shortage was serious. Unless they made much longer marches there was not enough to get them to Mount Hooper. This was 112 km away and they had kerosene for only five days. They ate frozen food part of the time and it took eight days to reach Mount Hooper.

They now admitted to themselves that they were all sick men, Oates being in the worst condition. He could no longer pull the sledge, but trudged behind as Evans had done towards the end. They were all so weak and tired they had stopped changing their clothes at night and it took them an hour and a half just to put on their footgear in the mornings.

On 17 March Scott wrote: 'I fear the crisis is very near now for poor Oates,' adding that he did not think that they would get past Mount Hooper, 'unless the dog-teams had replenished the Depot'. He had never asked that this should be done, though he had requested that the dog-teams should restore the depot at One Ton.

In two days they reached Mount Hooper and Scott wrote: 'The dogs that would have been our salvation have evidently failed'. As he wrote this, Cherry-Garrard and

Dmitri were at One Ton with the dog-teams, as Scott had requested.

On 11 March they discussed the possibility that they might not survive. The daily march was now never more than eleven kilometres and Oates knew that it was his weakness that was holding the others back. On 15 March he struggled out of his sleeping bag and left the tent.

'I am just going outside,' he said, 'and I may be some time.' He stumbled out on frostbitten feet into the blizzard, then fell while his life ebbed away in a frozen sleep.

Four days later the survivors made their last effort. They camped seventeen and a half kilometres from One Ton, with two days' food and one day's fuel. Now it was Scott who was the weakest.

It was agreed that Wilson and Bowers should set off next day, taking the sledge but leaving Scott in the tent. This meant a non-stop round march of thirty-five kilometres for without the tent they would not dare to rest. Even as they discussed it they knew the plan was impossible.

The attempt was never made, for next day a blizzard blew up and it was impossible to leave the tent. During the next nine days they slowly froze and starved to death. On 29 March Scott wrote: 'We shall stick it out to the end, but the end cannot be far. It seems a pity, but I do not think I can write more.' Under this he wrote: 'Last entry – for God's sake look after our people.'

18

The Second Season

TERRA NOVA left Cape Evans on 7 March 1912, since
there was a risk she would be frozen in if she stayed longer.
No one was really worried yet about the Polar Party, and
thirteen volunteers stayed on at the base to wait for them.
They were:

Dr Atkinson

Archer*	Debenham	Hooper	Nelson
Cherry-Garrard	Dmitri	Keohane	Williamson*
Crean	Gran	Lashly	Wright

* Volunteers from Terra Nova

Lieut. Evans would have been leader, but he was
invalided out as Shackleton had been in 1903. Most of the
scientific staff had contracted to come for one year only,
on leave from their regular appointments. Failing Lieut.
Evans, Lieut. Campbell should have been in charge, but
he was not at Cape Evans either.

His party had been picked up at their quarters near
Cape Adare on her way south, but landed again on the
coast of Victoria Land to continue the survey begun by
Professor David in 1908–09. They had   arranged to be
picked up by the ship during February, but had not
appeared at the rendezvous. So Campbell and his five
men were another missing party.

Hope was not given up for the Polar Party at Cape

Evans until the end of April, since they knew One Ton depot was well supplied, Cherry-Garrard having replenished it from the dog-sleds early in March. He and Dmitri had camped there for six days, hoping to be able to help the Polar Party over the last lap. Only the fact that they were running out of supplies had caused them to leave for the north, for it was no use restocking a depot if you stayed on and ate it bare yourselves.

When Cherry-Garrard arrived at Hut Point on 16 March he fully expected to find the Polar Party already there, for in the thickening weather they could very well have passed one another without noticing it. There had been few clear days that season and with the autumn the weather was worsening.

Terra Nova left for New Zealand, intending to make another attempt to pick up Campbell's party on the way, while Dr Anderson made another effort to meet the Polar Party. Hut Point was again cut off from Cape Evans until the sea froze again, and Atkinson, Cherry-Garrard, Dmitri and Keohane were marooned at the old base. They had the dog-teams, but these were exhausted after a season's hard work and needed a good rest.

On 22 March the dogs 'sang', as they always did at the approach of men. Thinking it was the Polar Party, the four left their breakfasts and searched for them. After two hours they had found nothing.

Three days later Dr Atkinson swore he had seen Campbell's party on the way in from Butter Point. Again, there was nothing. There was knocking on the windows and footsteps at the door that night, while both Dmitri and Keohane saw Campbell's men next day. The four at Hut Point were in a mood to snatch at straws and to see things that were not there.

Cherry-Garrard strained a tendon and could not walk, and Atkinson and Keohane set out on a forlorn hope to find Scott. They left on 27 March, two men hauling into the teeth of the wind, and their four-man tent was bitterly cold at nights with only two men in it. After three days Dr Atkinson realized that there was no hope of them getting to One Ton and that the Polar Party must have perished. He discussed the matter with Keohane, and they were back at Hut Point by 1 April.

Now they knew that the Polar Party would never walk in over the sea-ice, and they thought there was little chance they would ever see Campbell and his men again. One day Atkinson asked Cherry-Garrard:

'What about next year? Do we look for the Polar Party, or have a shot at rescuing Campbell?'

'Rescue Campbell, of course!' It seemed unthinkable at that time to look for dead men while there was a chance to rescue the living.

Gran, Williamson and Wright joined the four at Hut Point early in April, and one more effort was made to reach Campbell. Atkinson and three companions crossed to Butter Point on 15 April, there was only a few minutes of sunlight around noon each day and they travelled in twilight or darkness. They hoped they might meet Campbell's party sledging down the coast on the new sea-ice towards Cape Evans. They did not. They left a depot at Butter Point to assist a search-party in the spring.

They faced bitter conditions for six days, being almost in as bad a state as the Cape Crozier party of the year before on their return. This was on 13 April, the day they saw the sun for the last time before the spring. Two weeks later the sea-ice was firm for travelling and the party returned to Cape Evans with the weary dogs.

It was not a cheerful winter. The men at Cape Evans knew that somewhere to the south the Polar Party had perished, and that somewhere to the north six others were missing, with a faint chance of being alive. Apart from the two newcomers, men and dogs at Cape Evans were utterly spent.

It was not so warm in the hut, with only thirteen living there instead of twenty-six. Some of them were so exhausted that for a time they could only eat and sleep. Cherry-Garrard was in the worst shape and was relieved of all duties, except the production of the *South Polar Times* to be read around the table on Midwinter day.

There were mules in the stables this winter, brought down by *Terra Nova* as a gift from the Indian Government and trained as pack-animals for mountain warfare. They were willing little animals, but no better than the ponies had been crossing loose snow. They were the last hooved animals taken into the Antarctic for transport.

The men were reminded of their missing comrades twenty times a day. Scott's naval watch coat still hung on his cabin door, Dr Wilson's watercolours decorated the walls, they were using storelists in Bowers's neat writing, and some slept in sleeping bags stitched by P.O. Evans. While the stable smells and stamping of the mules brought back memories of Oates and the dead ponies.

But there was one great difference for the better, now problems were aired in the open, and freely discussed by all. The chief item of discussion was, of course, whom should they seek in the spring. In May some thought that one more effort should be made to find Campbell by a winter journey to Butter Point.

Against this it was argued that if exhausted men could

make the round trip from Cape Evans to Butter Point and back, then if Campbell had got so far he should be fit enough to do the last lap on his own. In any case, how did they know that Campbell had not been picked up by *Terra Nova* on her way to New Zealand? Or if this had not happened, that his party had found shelter and would be picked up by the ship as she came south? Finally it was decided that there was nothing to be done in that direction until next spring.

Then gradually they became convinced that there was only one thing to do during the next season – to search for the Polar Party, right up to the top of the Beardmore Glacier if necessary. There were those who thought this only a gesture, for no one imagined that the party had died on the trail. The most popular theory was that they had perished in the crevasses in the broken ice by the Cloudmaker and that their bodies would never be found.

No one wanted to face the Beardmore Glacier, especially the few who had been there before, and they had neither the men nor the means of going any distance on the plateau. There were only thirteen of them, there was very little in One Ton Depot, and the Search Journey would have to be planned from scratch. Nor could Cape Evans be left empty, for some would have to stay there to assist Campbell in case he turned up after all.

Dr Atkinson

Cherry-Garrard	Gran	Lashly	Wright
Crean	Hooper	Nelson	
Dmitri	Keohane	Williamson	

with seven mules and two dog-teams

This was the search party, which set out on 28 October and reached One Ton two weeks later, having averaged seventeen kilometres a day. The depot had not been opened since Cherry-Garrard had left it, indicating that the Polar Party had not got so far. It had been marked by a snow cairn topped with the kerosene can, from which the kerosene had vanished, though some had apparently soaked into the food below.

Next afternoon Wright saw something that might be a cairn to the east of the track, except that a cairn had no business to be where this object was. They crossed to have a look at it and someone idly kicked at the snow. This flaked away and under it lay the ventilator of a tent.

They dug down to the entrance, knowing something of what they must find, yet dreading to find it. Inside were the three bodies, Wilson and Bowers toggled up in their sleeping bags, Scott with his face exposed. By his side was a tin containing a wick cut from his finneskoe lacing, where he had burned the last of the primus lighting alcohol to warm his hands as he wrote in his Journal.

Dr Atkinson took the records, disturbing the bodies as little as possible, then collapsed the tent and read the burial service. A cairn was built over the grave and a cross made of Scott's ski set over this. Then they went on, to try and find Oates's body.

This was never found, for the winter snowfalls had drifted it deep down. Near the place where he had left the tent Atkinson read the burial service again and another cairn was raised. Sadly the party turned and travelled to the north.

The Search Party had their first good news for a year when they returned to Cape Evans to find Campbell and his party had arrived at last. At a time and place where fortitude was commonplace, they had perhaps shown the greatest fortitude of all.

After missing their appointment with *Terra Nova* they had set out to march down the coast to Cape Evans, but could not do so because of the rotten state of the sea-ice. They had a blubber stove, and were living largely off the country, as Professor David's party had done in 1908–09. Near Cape Drygalski they built an igloo, and slaughtered seals for the winter. They lived there until the spring, blackened with sooty blubber smoke, but otherwise in good health. As soon as the weather made it possible they travelled over the sea-ice the remaining 320 kilometres to Cape Evans.

Scott had drawn up a programme for a second season's field work, but Atkinson attempted no more journeys. Physically and emotionally the Cape Evans party were worn out. When *Terra Nova* arrived in January, the base at Cape Evans was closed down, and the expedition returned to civilization with the news of the Polar Party's deaths. The whole world knew of the tragedy by the end of February 1913.

This was not quite the end of the Heroic Age. Sir Douglas Mawson was in Adélie Land, but his expedition was basically different from the four described in this book. His was the first true scientific expedition, for Mawson was not seeking geographical 'firsts' or to make record-breaking journeys. He pioneered radio transmission in Antarctica, and by taking an aircraft fuselage mounted on ski can be said to have pioneered aviation. Mawson intended his 'air-tractor sledge' to haul supplies, but like Shackleton and Scott's motor tractors it was a failure. All the journeys in Adélie Land were done by muscle power.

Sir Ernest Shackleton launched the last and most ambitious expedition of the era, and it failed. It involved two ships, one to make a landing on an absolutely unknown coast in the Weddell Sea, the other to sail the now well-known track to McMurdo Sound. Both were to land parties for the winter. At the Ross Sea side of the continent depots were to be laid over the Ice Shelf to the Beardmore Glacier, to assist the party from the Weddell Sea, who were to march over the continent, across the Pole to McMurdo Sound and so back to civilization.

It does not seem possible that it could have succeeded, but Shackleton was a remarkable man and a wonderful leader and if anyone could have done this terrific feat at that time it was he. In fact, the expedition never started. Shackleton failed to reach the coast at the Weddell Sea, and his ship, *Endurance*, was crushed and destroyed by the ice. The story of how he and his crew escaped, without the loss of a man and after months of camping on a drifting ice floe, is one of the most thrilling tales in the English language.

Misfortune dogged this expedition, for the second ship was beset by ice in McMurdo Sound, and was held for months before being freed. As an account of fortitude and endurance the record of the Trans-Polar Expedition makes thrilling reading, but it was too ambitious. It got nowhere and achieved nothing, and did Shackleton's reputation a great deal of harm.

Even had he landed on the Weddell Sea coast Shackleton would have almost certainly failed to cross the continent on foot with dog transport. When the crossing of Antarctica was achieved by the Fuchs-Hillary Expedition during the International Geophysical Year of 1957–58 this could not have been done without the use of field radio and supply-drops by aircraft, and the presence of a semi-permanent American Base at the South Pole itself.

19

The Scott-Amundsen Controversy

AMUNDSEN'S SUCCESS was known in 1912, but Scott's fate remained a mystery until the following year. In Britain the Scott tragedy overshadowed the Norwegian achievement, and many behaved as though Amundsen were somehow responsible for the deaths of the English Polar Party. It would be nearer the truth to say that Scott and Amundsen both gambled their lives on the chance of reaching the South Pole and that Amundsen won.

The apparent ease of his journey does not mean that it was a simple task. Amundsen took great risks from the time of his arrival in the Ross Sea. He took a risk when he built Framheim at the Bay of Whales, where it might have become part of a drifting iceberg before he even started for the Pole. He took an even greater risk in gambling on the chance of finding a second pass through the mountains south of the Ross Ice Shelf. Until he found it the Axel Heiberg Glacier was unknown, and Amundsen had planned his journey as if it were a certainty.

Amundsen's critics made much of the fact that his base at Framheim was ninety-six kilometres nearer to the Pole than was Cape Evans. But the base at Cape Evans was absolutely secure, and the country around it quite well known. Being closer to the Pole at the Bay of Whales would not have helped Amundsen if the ice had broken out, or the Axel Heiberg glacier had not been where it was.

Amundsen was also criticized for the manner in which he employed dogs, first as transport and then killing them for food. Dogs are used for transport in a number of places, and are still so used in polar regions. Scott and Shackleton both used dogs, but were never criticized for doing so.

Dogs have been bred for meat by at least two peoples – the American Indian and the Chinese – and while we in Europe do not do this it is really a matter of taste. After all, we breed pigs for the sole purpose of eating them, and the pig is an intelligent animal.

Shackleton and Scott used ponies both for transport and food, but were never criticized for this. None of the ponies they took survived the journey. Amundsen brought back eleven dogs from the Pole, which were pensioned off and lived out the rest of their lives in Norway. In his treatment of animals Amundsen compares very favourably with Scott, who brought no dogs back from his first polar journeys and killed and ate his ponies on the second.

There must have been almost as many books written about Scott as there have about James Cook, and for many years it was near heresy to question Scott or his methods. Any mistakes he made were glossed over by the tragedy of the deaths of his party. The death of Oates in particular is held up to this day as an example of great self-sacrifice. But, were any of them really necessary?

One difference between Amundsen and Scott was that Amundsen was a professional explorer, who had prepared for this way of life from boyhood and had done nothing else for sixteen years. Scott was not a professional, but used Antarctic exploration to help advance his naval career.

The *Discovery* Expedition was a success. Scott made mistakes, but he appeared to learn from them and on this first expedition he did not make the same mistake twice. He pioneered methods of living and travelling in a region as hostile to man as the surface of the moon.

He was decorated and promoted to captain in the navy and seemed reasonably certain, in the state of naval expansion at the time, to become a rear-admiral in the normal way of promotion. But this was not certain, and Scott needed a certainty. To make sure of his naval future he formed a second expedition to Antarctica.

He was a different man on this expedition. He made some of the same mistakes as he had on his first, and some he made more than once. Taken singly none but the last of these would have killed him, but collectively they all had an effect.

The first mistake was to mix his transport. Taking tractors was a mistake, for in an expedition where transport is so important there is no place to act as a proving ground for machinery. Machinery may be tested to destruction in sub-arctic Canada, in temperatures as low as any endured at Cape Evans, and carried to the proving ground by railway. This was so in Scott's day as it is now. There was no need to clutter the ship with tons of unwieldy deck cargo over the stormiest seas in the world.

Dogs *or* ponies, not ponies *and* dogs. Scott knew that mixed man-dog teams were not a success, and from a study of Shackleton's *Heart of the Antarctic* he should have learned of the difference between pony and dog pace. (We know that Scott used this book to plan his Polar Journey, for he refers to it constantly in his Journal, and a copy exists with scribbled notes in his writing in the margins.)

A second mistake was in planning for two bases. This led to overloading the ship, thus straining the hull and causing leaks, and was at least partly responsible for the failure of the pumps. The passage from New Zealand to the Ross Sea in a small ship can rarely be a pleasure cruise, but Scott severely overworked his shore party and made it a purgatory for all hands.

The third mistake was in making too early a start. There was evidence fully available to Scott that nothing is gained by entering the pack-ice before the last week in December, and by starting when he did Scott gained only three days over *Nimrod*'s time for 1909 at the expense of three weeks' consumption of coal. Conditions in 1902 and 1911 must have been similar, for *Fram* and *Discovery* entered the pack on the same day and both took only four days to get through to the Ross Sea.

The fourth mistake was in underestimating the work necessary to unload the ship and set up a base. This was something Scott had not done before, because he had allowed *Discovery* to be frozen in and the huts and stores to be unloaded at leisure, some not until the second year.

His fifth mistake was to rely too much on the willing volunteer. Some men overworked themselves to a degree that should never have been permitted. During the un-loading most of the shore-party worked a seventeen-hour day seven days a week, with snatched meals and little sleep. Thirteen of these men set out on the Depot Journey before the unloading was finished and one of them, Bowers, had not slept for three days before setting out. Only by a series of miracles did the Depot Journey not end in tragedy.

Meanwhile, a few of the scientific staff did little more than get their equipment ashore and begin their re-searches, while the ship's company worked regular watches, with sleep and meals at regular intervals. As

Cherry-Garrard says: 'Men did too much, were told they had done too much, but nothing was done about it.'

His sixth mistake was about diet. There was no scurvy at the base on this expedition, probably due to the liberal use of fresh seal and penguin meat and the drinking of that well-known naval antiscorbutic, lime juice. Yet Scott did nothing about any antiscorbutic in the sledge diet, which he proposed to live on for at least four months. Lime juice could have been allowed to freeze into blocks, and would have added little to the weight carried. Or cod-liver oil and malt, often given to children to fortify the winter diet, could have been used. The necessary dose is small, and again the extra weight would have been negligible.

His seventh mistake was to rely on ponies instead of dogs. With dogs he could have made an earlier start, for although Amundsen did not begin his main journey until the third week in October he made a depot journey in September five weeks earlier. This was six weeks before Scott could face the trail with his ponies. If he had used the dogs he had to advance One Ton Depot to where he first intended to place it, 80° south, he could have lived to reach the base.

His eighth mistake was in sending Meares back with the dogs from the foot of the Beardmore. Cherry-Garrard did not think dogs could have climbed it, but the Axel Heiberg is short, steeper and just as high, and Amundsen's dogs climbed it. If dogs can climb one there seems no reason why they should not climb the other. If Scott had used dogs to the top of the glacier the men would have been so much fresher for the final man-hauling stage.

His ninth mistake was to command the expedition as if it were a battleship, and he was only approachable through his Heads of Departments. These were Lieut.

Evans (Administration), Lieut. Bowers (Supply), Captain Oates (Transport) and Dr Wilson (Scientific Staff). Professor Griffith Taylor has said that he never once spoke to Scott after his first interview. Everything had to be arranged through Wilson or the other Heads of Departments.

His tenth mistake was to ignore the advice of experts. An instance of this was the time on the first depot journey when Scott ignored Oates's advice to shoot a pony and feed the meat to the dogs. This pony died later and the meat was lost.

Taken singularly, none of these errors would have proved fatal, for it was the eleventh mistake that killed them all. This was when, on the Polar Plateau, he split the last two carefully planned four-man trail units into unequal parties of five and three. All five died of scurvy, the last four having the condition aggravated by hunger and lack of fuel.

The last three died at a point only seventeen kilometres from One Ton Depot, where fresh food that might have saved their lives was waiting. Over the last five weeks they had suffered from a constant shortage of fuel. Two days after the parties separated on the Plateau Scott noted in his Journal that it was taking half an hour a day longer to cook for five than it had done to cook for four.

(This does not mean that it would have taken half an hour less to cook for three in Lieut. Evans's party, for the same mass of cold metal had to be heated in each case. Any difference in time might be so little that Evans would not notice it.)

Until P.O. Evans died the Polar Party were a five-man team forty-four days in all, travelling on thirty-seven of these. If the extra half-hour of cooking time had been spent in travel at only one kilometre an hour they could have covered thirty kilometres more than they did, and so have reached the depot at One Ton.

Or this could be reckoned as a saving of fuel – saving half an hour of fuel each day for forty-four days amounts to twenty-two hours of fuel supply. This extra fuel could have saved their lives and the shortages in the depots would not have mattered so much. In fact, they might not even have been noticed.

The supporting parties were never accused of taking more than their share of fuel from the depots, but the inference was there. During the second season this inference was very firmly scotched when a sealed case of eight one-gallon cans of kerosene was dug out at the base. Three cans were full, two partly so, and three were empty.

The cans were coloured dark red, sealed with a leather washer and a screw cap. The kerosene was a special blend, made up to vaporize readily at low temperatures. It was usual to mark the depots with a snow cairn, topped with the kerosene can as an extra marker. In clear weather the dark red can showed for miles against the white background.

During the Antarctic summer it is daylight right through the twenty-four hours. As the sun circled the horizon each side of the can would be heated in turn, sufficiently to vaporize a little of the contents, though the opposite side of the can might be coated with frost. Cold could make the leather washer shrink, so that it ceased to be a seal and the precious fuel escaped.

Was Scott too old for the task? He was forty-three, which many consider to be the best years of a man's life. Many consider that this depends on the man and the nature of the work. For some sports an athlete is too old at thirty and many academics consider a scientist or scholar may do his best work in his mid-twenties. In his early thirties Scott had shown he was a fine explorer and an inspired leader.

On his second expedition he seemed to think less clearly. He should have seen that the two-base project was too ambitious to be set up from one ship. The near suicidal journey to Cape Crozier in the first winter should have either been banned or better organized, and the time Scott took in the spring would have been better spent setting One Ton Depot further to the south. On the return from the Pole he had a fixed impression that Mount Hooper was to be replenished by the dog-teams, but he has given no orders on this subject at all.

Was Scott ruthless enough? He disliked the killing of animals and never did so personally. The inclusion of Wilson in the Polar Party was pure sentiment, not to be excused on the pretext that Wilson was a doctor. They were in a situation where nothing could be done for the most serious ailment except the simplest first-aid.

Was sheer physical fatigue a responsible factor? Dr Atkinson thought Scott might have become too tired to think clearly, for he had done some research into the physical effects of man-hauled sledges. Dr Atkinson found that the total physical strength of a man remained the same, granting he was well fed and fit, but the arms declined in strength by as much as 70 per cent as the legs and back adapted themselves to pulling in harness. This would account for the arm and back work involved in making and breaking camp becoming more tiring the longer men were out on the trail.

Were the Polar Party affected by cold and lack of oxygen? Undoubtedly by cold, and possibly by lack of oxygen too. Altitude can slow mental processes, which has been proved by tests carried out in decompression chambers.

Scott realized he had made a mistake in splitting the party into two unequal groups, and admitted it when he made the Journal entry about the extra time taken up by the cooking. Had he lived to work up his notes into a book as good as *Voyage of the 'Discovery'* he would almost certainly have admitted this. He paid for the mistake with five lives.

There had been no war for some years, and a popular hero was needed in England. Oates and Scott passed into legend, and once this happens all the mistakes are wiped out and it becomes almost a heresy to examine the facts.

It is admittedly easy to be wise after the event, but there is nothing mentioned in this book, except the details of Amundsen's polar journey, that was not known to Scott. Amundsen on reaching the Ross Sea had no local knowledge that was denied to Scott. Scott knew about the Beardmore Glacier and planned to use it. Amundsen did not know what he might find south of the Ice Shelf, only that he would have to make the best of whatever it was. The chances of success in the midwinter of 1911 were heavily in favour of Scott.

But Scott kept on making mistakes and the last one killed him and his companions. After studying the evidence, one is forced to the conclusion it was a 'Tragedy of Errors'.

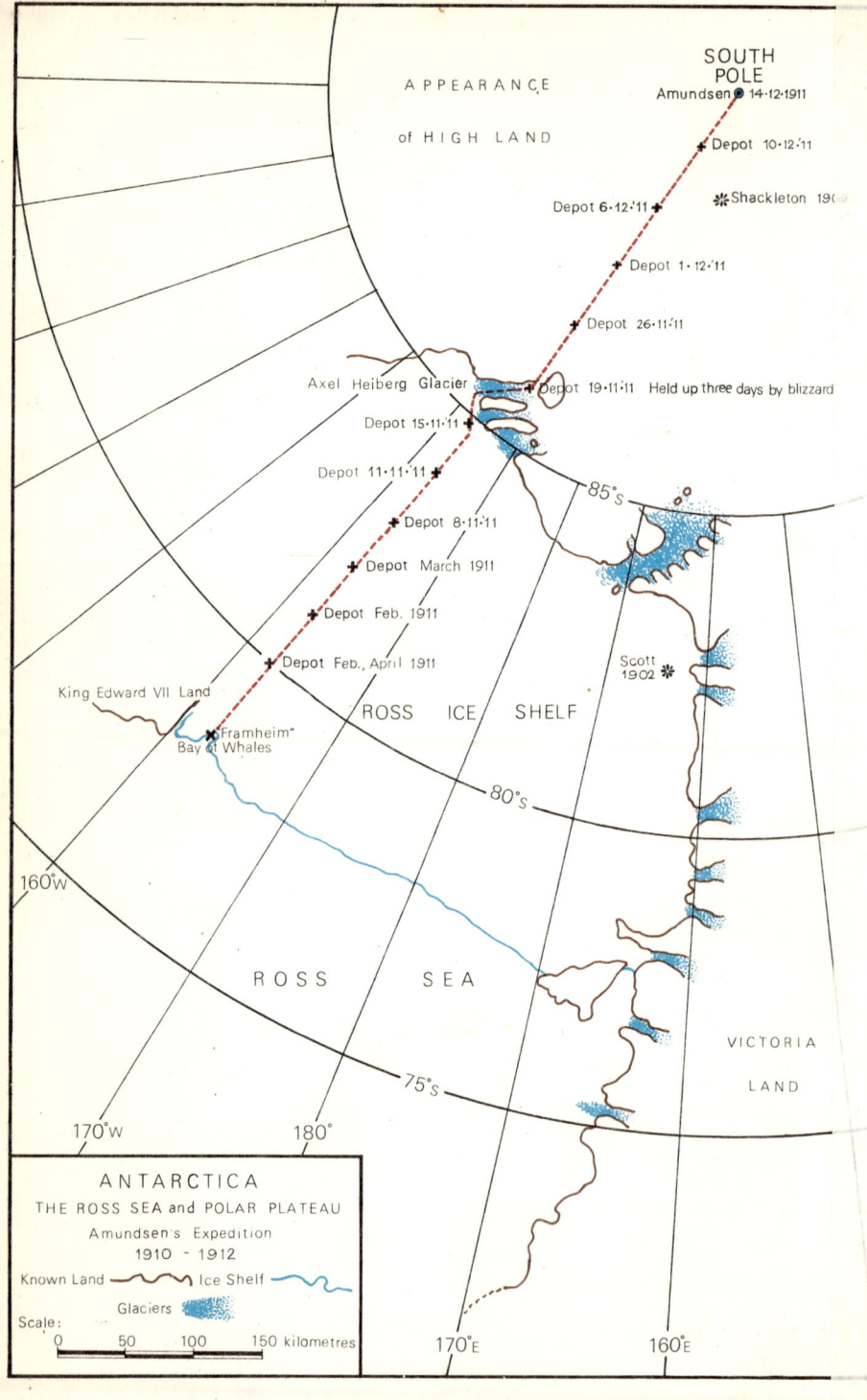

SOUTH POLE
Amundsen● 14·12·1911

APPEARANCE
of HIGH LAND

+ Depot 10·12·'11

❊ Shackleton 190

Depot 6·12·11 +

+ Depot 1·12·'11

+ Depot 26·11·'11

Axel Heiberg Glacier ·····Depot 19·11·'11   Held up three days by blizzard

85°S

Depot 15·11·11 +

Depot 11·11·'11 +

+ Depot 8·11·'11

+ Depot March 1911

+ Depot Feb. 1911

Scott 1902 ❊

+ Depot Feb., April 1911

King Edward VII Land

×"Framheim"
Bay of Whales

ROSS   ICE   SHELF

80°S

160°W

ROSS   SEA

VICTORIA

LAND

75°S

170°W   180°   170°E   160°E

ANTARCTICA
THE ROSS SEA and POLAR PLATEAU
Amundsen's Expedition
1910 – 1912

Known Land ∿∿∿   Ice Shelf ∿∿∿

Glaciers

Scale:
0   50   100   150 kilometres